Reaching Out to Africa's Orphans:
A Framework for Public Action

Reaching Out to Africa's Orphans: A Framework for Public Action

Kalanidhi Subbarao
Diane Coury

THE WORLD BANK
Washington, D.C.

© 2004 The International Bank for Reconstruction and Development / The World Bank
1818 H Street, NW
Washington, DC 20433
Telephone: 202-473-1000
Internet: www.worldbank.org
E-mail: feedback@worldbank.org

ISBN 08213-5857-X

Library of Congress Cataloging-in-Publication data has been applied for.

Cover Photo: World Bank Photo Library

Contents

Tables

Figures

Boxes

Foreword

The human immunodeficiency virus (HIV) and the acquired immunodeficiency syndrome (AIDS) are generating a major humanitarian crisis for families in Sub-Saharan Africa. The number of children who have lost one or both parents to AIDS is expected to rise to 35 million by 2010. Rolling back decades of progress in social development, HIV/AIDS has become a major constraint in the fight against poverty. Moreover, many African countries are suffering from civil unrest and from postconflict situations, which are producing even more orphans and displaced children.

As the number of affected children has escalated, the risk of orphanhood has quickly transformed itself from a shock that randomly affects families to a more systemic shock that has had adverse effects on whole communities and countries, threatening the realization of the United Nations' Millennium Development Goals for education, health, nutrition, and poverty reduction.

The World Bank has broadened its efforts to address the HIV/AIDS crisis in all of its dimensions. This study is aimed at addressing the needs of young children affected by the loss of one or both parents as a consequence of HIV/AIDS and conflicts. In doing so, it makes a substantial contribution to our understanding of the many risks and vulnerabilities faced by orphans and the ameliorating role played by governments and donors.

The study brings together the admittedly limited evidence from interventions in behalf of orphans with a view toward advancing our knowledge on what works and what does not in mitigating the risks faced by orphans and in enhancing the capacities of communities to address this problem. It also pulls together the information on the costs and cost-effectiveness of the ongoing interventions being implemented by various agencies. Juxtaposing the risks and needs of orphans against the effectiveness (including cost-effectiveness) of care-giving arrangements, the study addresses issues bearing on how to scale up the more promising of the interventions.

The authors draw several important conclusions on the strengths and weaknesses of various programs, targeting methods, and their implications, and in particular highlight the gaps in our knowledge on the cost-effectiveness of interventions and the potential incentive effects of orphan care. Considering that resources are limited and the problem is immense, the study rightly underscores the need for coordination of efforts among all agencies seeking to respond to the crisis.

As the authors point out, there is as yet no established "blueprint" for action in behalf of orphans, and this study does not pretend to offer one. Its modest aim is to collate and organize the available evidence and contribute to a better understanding of what kinds of interventions and approaches might work in a given country situation, and thus offer some guidance to all agencies involved in responding to the crisis of orphans in Sub-Saharan Africa.

Robert Holzmann
Sector Director (Social Protection)
Human Development Network

Oey Astra Meesook
Sector Director, Human Development
Africa Region

Acknowledgments

The authors benefited from guidance and early interactions with Margaret Grosh, Keith Hansen, and Arvil Van Adams. Peer reviewers were Peter Mcdermott, Menahem Prywes, and John Williamson. John Williamson not only provided detailed comments, but also generously shared numerous reports and documents bearing on the subject. Alok Bhargava, Hans Binswanger, Mark Connolly, Laura Frigenti, Anne Kielland, Viviana Mangiaterra, Brian Ngo, Susan Opper, and participants in a Workshop on Orphans and Vulnerable Children held at the World Bank on May 14–15, 2003, provided comments on an earlier draft.

The authors also wish to thank colleagues at UNICEF, the U.S. Agency for International Development, World Vision, and Save the Children for their advice and interactions. For unfailing support and encouragement, the authors wish to express their gratitude to Arvil Van Adams, Keith Hansen, Robert Holzmann, and Oey Astra Meesook. The study was financed at the World Bank by the President's Contingency Fund for Orphans and Vulnerable Children and the Africa Region (Human Development).

The findings, interpretations, and conclusions expressed in this study are entirely those of the authors. They do not necessarily represent the view of the World Bank, its executive directors, or the countries they represent.

The publication of the study is generously supported by the Norwegian Trust Fund for Education. The authors are grateful to Manorama Rani for preparing the manuscript for publication.

Reader's Guide and Executive Summary

The purpose of this study is to provide an overview of the issues pertaining to orphans and vulnerable children (OVC) and, based on the available evidence on interventions, offer some guidelines on the approaches and interventions that best mitigate or cope with the many risks and vulnerabilities confronted by them. To date, there is no package of established knowledge describing how to intervene in behalf of OVC, what kind of assistance is needed, and how to channel it. This study does not pretend, however, to offer that "package" of established knowledge. Its aim is more modest: to collate and organize the available bits and pieces of information from diverse sources on the profile of risks faced by OVC and on the costs and pros and cons of interventions, and then to offer some guidance on what kinds of intervention or approaches might work in a given country context or situation.

The study begins by stressing three points. First, the number of orphans is growing at an alarming rate, and therefore the vulnerabilities associated with orphanhood require immediate attention. Second, because resources are limited and not all orphans are in need of assistance, there is an urgent need to target assistance to the neediest children in a nonstigmatizing fashion, within the framework of the present limited knowledge of what works and what does not. Third, although there is still no blueprint on the best way to scale up interventions, the World Bank's multicountry AIDS programs (MAPs) do offer an opportunity not only to pilot assistance efforts but also to extend assistance to as many of the needy as possible, albeit seeking interagency coordination of efforts both to avoid duplication of efforts and to learn from the experience of everyone involved in this effort. *An important rationale for such an intervention is to ensure that orphans' human development (access to health care and education) is not in any way jeopardized.* Clearly, the challenge faced by all stakeholders and donors in channeling assistance to the affected children is enormous.

An important first step is to assess the risks faced by orphans and their specific requirements, which vary a great deal depending on the situation in which these children find themselves. These risks range from economic and social risks to psychological risks and trauma. Available evidence on the magnitude of the orphan problem and the diverse nature of the risks are reviewed in chapter 1. The approach relies on a risks/needs analysis, which strongly complements the right approach.

Because risk patterns differ across orphans even within a sociocultural environment, it is important to carefully assess those needs that emanate from their vulnerabilities. For example, after the death of the breadwinner in a household, the immediate risk could be a precipitous shortfall in per capita consumption, driving even an otherwise nonpoor household into poverty. Or a child, especially a girl, could be withdrawn from school. Or a child, though food needs are met, might not be able to bear the psychological trauma and so might need immediate counseling.

Understanding the risks of orphans and vulnerable children is critical for attaining the Millennium Development Goals set by the United Nations for education, health, nutrition, and poverty. The reason is that the exposure of these children to risks has a critical impact on the school enrollments, health, and nutritional status of several million vulnerable children. Therefore, prior to launching any intervention in their behalf, agencies and organizations must ensure that they are aware of these children's risks and needs (which vary a great deal across countries), and, to the extent possible, they must design interventions in such a way as to help orphans and vulnerable children attain the Millennium Development Goals for education, health, nutrition, and poverty. The risks facing and the needs of vulnerable children are addressed in chapter 2.

Once the needs and demand patterns become clear, it is time to ask: who are the caregivers (on the supply side)? The available evidence is reviewed in chapter 3. Again, countries differ widely on the nature of caregivers and their strengths and weaknesses. For example, countries vary a great deal in their community capacity, which in turn differs, at least in part, according to the magnitude of the problem. In countries adversely affected by the orphan crisis such as Uganda, a widespread network of national and international nongovernmental agencies devoted to orphan welfare has emerged. Yet even in Uganda, the magnitude of the problem is such that a vast number of institutions and agencies are able to meet the needs of only 5–10 percent of the affected children. Prior to launching any intervention, then, an organization or agency must know the nature of the networks in operation, the variety of caring arrangements prevalent in the country, and their strengths and weaknesses, and assess whether a community has reached its limit in caring for OVC. This overview is provided in chapter 3, which also describes a quick-and-dirty methodology for assessing community capacity.

Once the risks and needs of OVC and the nature of care-giving arrangements prevalent in a country have been assessed, the next step is to ask: what can be done, by way of public policy, to strengthen the community coping capacity and the existing community-driven care-giving arrangements. For example, if the problem is one of a sharp fall in consumption and the threat is a poverty trap, what interventions could augment a household's income-earning capacity after the death of the principal breadwinner? The nature of interventions and the various ways in which public action could strengthen community action are reviewed in chapter 4.

A variety of interventions have been put in place by communities, nongovernmental organizations (NGOs), and governments to address a range of risks and vulnerabilities faced by orphans and vulnerable children in Sub-Saharan Africa. The interventions vary by the scope (i.e., how many children are assisted) and the type of care or assistance provided (such as school and nutrition support, tracing the extended family, or group home), and its quality. The enormous variety in interventions and the differences in their scale of operation, as well as assessments of varying quality, make it difficult to come up with cost norms for different types of interventions. Chapter 5 outlines the methodological difficulties of cost comparisons. Subject to the limitations discussed at length, the chapter provides the best judgment possible as of today of the costs associated with various interventions. But these estimates must be regarded as tentative; clearly, more robust information than is currently available is needed for understanding the cost-effectiveness of various interventions. The broad conclusion of this chapter is that community-driven interventions at the household level appear to be the most cost-effective, and formal orphanages appear to be prohibitively expensive. Within these two extremes are a number of intermediary options with varying costs, and these options are reviewed in chapter 5.

The most difficult issue in providing assistance to OVC is how to scale up and replicate an intervention that has proved successful and cost-effective when operated on a small scale in a given country. Scaling up necessarily implies confronting three issues on the inputs side: (a) the costs of scaling up and the financial capacity of governments, (b) the organizational/institutional capabilities and community-level resources, and (c) the definitive evidence that a particular program intervention has a proven track record of success and thus is worthy of scaling up. In other words, anyone attempting to expand should know first *who* to focus on, *what* to focus on, and the *capacity* (financial/institutional) to deliver the program. There is still no blueprint to how best to scale up and replicate interventions. However, a community-driven development initiative offers an important window of opportunity to scale up efforts by devolving funds to communities and local authorities and empowering them to launch protective programs in behalf of orphans and vulnerable children. Chapter 6 provides an illustrative road map of the kinds of issues that one needs to confront, underscoring the point that much depends on the individual country situation.

Learning from experience is one important component of any planned intervention on behalf of OVC. But that learning process depends critically on monitoring and evaluation. One reason for the difficulty, noted earlier, in assessing the impacts and costs of past and ongoing interventions is that most institutions that have sponsored interventions to protect orphans have not kept credible monitoring and evaluation systems in place. A brief introduction to the issues surrounding establishment of a good monitoring and evaluation system for OVC interventions, including the challenges and information requirements, is provided in chapter 7.

Although we hope readers will read this entire study, it is hoped that this short reader's guide will, in addition to providing a glimpse at the full contents of the study, guide task managers to the specific chapter of most critical importance to a given country situation.

CHAPTER 1

Orphans and Vulnerable Children: An Introduction

This study describes the risks and vulnerabilities faced by orphans and vulnerable children (OVC) in Africa and the interventions being undertaken by governments, donors, and nongovernmental organizations (NGOs). The study is directed mainly at the task team leaders (TTLs) of the World Bank's multicountry AIDS programs (MAPs),[1] the line ministries in client countries charged with protecting vulnerable children, and the donor agencies and NGOs that have programs in support of orphans and vulnerable children.

Defining and Identifying Vulnerable Children

In this study, vulnerable children are defined as those *whose safety, well-being, and development are, for various reasons, threatened.* Of the many factors that accentuate children's vulnerabilities, the most important are lack of care and affection, adequate shelter, education, nutrition, and psychological support.[2] Although children exposed to many facets of deprivation and poverty are vulnerable, children who have lost their parents may be particularly vulnerable, because they do not have the emotional and physical maturity to address adequately and bear the psychological trauma associated with parental loss. A checklist of children's vulnerabilities and indicators thereof, disaggregated by gender and age, appears in appendix B (table B.1).

Because the definition just given of vulnerable children is very broad and encompasses a huge proportion of children, it is difficult to apply in the field. In addition, because resources are limited, those working in this area have to rely on very specific approaches and focus on the most critically vulnerable children. One way to implement this strategy is to think about the problem in relative terms. In this framework, orphans and vulnerable children could be defined as *those children who are most at risk of facing increased negative outcomes compared with the "average" child in their society.* The main negative outcomes are, among other things, severe malnutrition, above-average rates of morbidity and mortality, lower-than-average rates of school attendance and completion at the primary level, and, in all probability, a heavier work burden (both paid and unpaid child labor).

Risk and Vulnerability

The degree and type of vulnerability faced by children are shaped by the risk and stress characteristics (i.e., magnitude, frequency, duration, and history) to which they (but also households and communities) are exposed, and these tend to vary between countries and over time (Holzmann and Jorgensen 2000; Heitzmann, Canagarajah, and Siegel 2002). Table 1.1 lists examples of risks by categories. From this table, one can infer that a family breakup will certainly not induce the same type of vulnerabilities in children as a flood, a war, or an HIV/AIDS epidemic. Similarly, the level of HIV prevalence within a region will shape the degree of vulnerabilities faced by children, as will the phase of the epidemic.[3]

The conjunction of different risks may trigger further vulnerability for children. For example, a drought may increase the probability that an orphan will suffer a higher rate of severe malnutrition than nonorphan children in the same region and orphans living in a region not affected by drought. Furthermore, vulnerability is shaped by the type and level of assets possessed.[4] Indeed, a person's level of vulnerability (or a household's or a community's) is determined by its risk–asset balance. Thus children's vulnerability generally, and orphans' vulnerability

Table 1.1 Examples of Risks to Children, by Category

Category of risks	Examples
Natural	Heavy rainfall, landslides, volcanic eruptions, earthquakes, floods, hurricanes, droughts, strong winds
Health	Illness, injury, accidents, disability, epidemics (e.g., malaria, HIV/AIDS), famines
Life cycle	Birth, maternity, old age, family breakup, orphanhood
Social	Crime, domestic violence, terrorism, gangs, war, social upheaval
Economic	Unemployment, harvest failure, business failure, resettlement, output collapse, balance-of-payment shock, financial crisis, currency crisis
Political	Discrimination, riots, political unrest, coup d'état
Environmental	Pollution, deforestation, land degradation, nuclear disaster

Source: Adapted from Heitzmann, Canagarajah, and Siegel (2002), based on Holzmann and Jorgensen (2000).

particularly, is very context-specific and must be analyzed within the sociocultural milieu in which children live.

Bearing in mind the sociocultural, economic, and country context, one could include the following under the rubric of orphans and vulnerable children: orphans, abandoned children, street children, handicapped children, child soldiers and those affected by war (displaced and refugees), children exposed to hazardous work, children who are victims of trafficking and various forms of abuse and neglect, and children living in extremely poor conditions. These groups, far from being exclusive, may actually overlap. All these types of children are vulnerable in the sense that they face a great risk of not being raised in an environment conducive to an appropriate physical and mental development because of exposure to the vulnerabilities listed in table B.1 of appendix B.

Defining these categories of vulnerable children more narrowly is difficult because of differences across countries and cultures. However, some general guidelines on defining the various categories of OVC can be derived from the existing literature:

• *Orphan* usually refers to a child under the age of 18 years (or 15 years) whose mother (maternal orphan) or father (paternal orphan) or both (double orphan) are dead. Although AIDS is the major cause of death among adults in much of Sub-Saharan Africa, it is totally inappropriate to distinguish orphans by the nature of the death of their parents (such as AIDS orphans). Distinguishing AIDS orphans from other orphans only increases the stigma and discrimination the children orphaned by AIDS are already facing.[5]

- *Street child* is one who has no home, or one who is forced to work or spend extensive time in public spaces, or both.

- *Child laborer under strenuous work* refers to a child involved in some form of hazardous and exploitative economic activity (and below the legal age established by the country's legislation).

- *Child soldier* refers to "any person under 18 years of age who is a member of or attached to the armed forces or an armed group, whether or not there is an armed conflict. Child soldiers may perform tasks ranging from direct participation in combat; military activities such as scouting, spying, sabotage, acting as decoys, couriers or guards; training, drill and other preparations; support functions such as portering and domestic tasks; sexual slavery and forced labour" (http://www.us-childsoldiers.org/tehp.html).

- *Disabled child* is one whose abilities to perform a normal human activity are restricted.

As stressed earlier, the type of vulnerability faced by children is strongly contextual. Because risk patterns tend to differ from one setting to another, so will the vulnerabilities and, as a result, the type of OVC. In countries with high prevalence rates of HIV/AIDS such as those in southern Africa (e.g., Malawi, South Africa, Uganda, and Zimbabwe), orphans, children whose parents are chronically ill (and who are likely to be HIV-positive), children infected with HIV/AIDS, and children living in households that have taken orphans are particularly vulnerable (World Vision 2002). In conflict or postconflict settings (e.g., Angola, Rwanda, and Sierra Leone), vulnerable children will be found among child soldiers, internally displaced and refugee children, sexually harmed children, orphans, and abandoned children. In countries facing natural disasters such as drought, children of families resorting to distress migration (in search of food and fodder for animals) may be particularly vulnerable to nutritional stress and loss of schooling. In some countries, the situation can be mixed—for example, in Burundi, Eritrea, Ethiopia, Rwanda, and Sierra Leone, child vulnerability ranges from orphanhood to malnutrition and disability.

Understanding the risks of orphans and vulnerable children is critical to attaining the United Nations' Millennium Development Goals (MDGs) set for education, health, nutrition, and poverty, because those risks have a critical effect on the school enrollments, health, and nutritional status of several million vulnerable children. The probability of not attaining the MDGs is particularly high for children located in countries experiencing risk compounding—that is, an orphan who lives in a country emerging from years of civil conflict and subjected to a severe covariate shock such as drought might face multiple risks and be very vulnerable to dropping out of school compared with another orphan placed in a country facing fewer overall challenges. Therefore, before launching any intervention on their behalf, donor agencies and others should be aware of the risks and needs (which vary a great deal across countries) and, to the extent possible, design interventions in such a way as to ensure that orphans and vulnerable children benefit from attainment of the Millennium Development Goals for education, health, nutrition, and poverty.

In the prevailing environment of widespread deprivation and poverty in most countries of Sub-Saharan Africa, the numbers of orphans and vulnerable children are growing: estimates suggest that the number of orphans alone (double and single orphans from all causes of parental death) was 34 million in 2001 (UNAIDS 2002). Even in the best of circumstances, reaching all the OVC is not feasible.[6] In many country situations, it may be necessary to identify those children among the OVC who are the most in need. But one cannot identify the needy children without knowing their potential or ex ante risk patterns. Indeed, identifying these risk patterns is far more important than determining how many orphans there are in a given country, because often the numbers may not tell the whole story. In some countries, the numbers may not be high, but the uninsured risks faced by children may be large, in which case potentially marginalized orphans may eventually become street children, child laborers, or victims of child trafficking. In other settings or country contexts, the risks of orphanhood may not be that serious; indeed, in some countries the poverty-induced vulnerability among children could be even greater than the vulnerabilities associated with orphanhood.

This Study: A Focus on Orphans

The study described in this volume focuses mainly on orphans (i.e., those children under the age of 18 years who have lost either one or both parents from any cause) in HIV/AIDS-affected zones, although we are conscious of the fact that many other children who are not orphans have been made vulnerable by the spread of HIV/AIDS, wars, or other shocks. However, we believe that the general principles and analysis contained in the following chapters will be relevant for most OVC.[7] The main reason for our focus on orphans is that since the rapid spread of HIV/AIDS, orphans have become an increasingly large and visible potentially vulnerable group in much of Sub-Saharan Africa.[8] In fact, of the 34 million orphans (double and single) from any cause estimated for 2001, 11 million were attributed to AIDS (figure 1.1).[9]

In many countries, the HIV epidemic has not yet reached its peak,[10] and so the number of children rendered vulnerable by the disease is

Figure 1.1 Number and Proportion of Orphans Up to Age 14 in Sub-Saharan Africa, 1990–2010

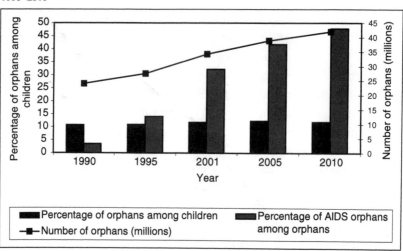

Source: UNAIDS (2002).

expected to increase. Moreover, because of the long incubation period of the disease (8–10 years), the adverse impacts of HIV/AIDS on children, households, and communities will linger for decades after the epidemic begins to wane. According to Levine and Foster (2000, cited by Foster and Williamson 2000), the mortality rates will not reach a plateau until 2020, which means that the number of orphaned children will remain high at least until 2030. Simulations show that by 2010 the number of orphans and AIDS orphans will be 42 million and 20 million, respectively (UNAIDS 2002). Thus by 2010 between 14 and 25 percent of *all* children in 11 out of 15 countries of eastern and southern Africa will be orphaned, of whom between 50 and 89 percent will be orphaned because of AIDS (figure 1.1). In Zimbabwe, for example, 22 percent (1.3 million) of children are expected to be orphaned by 2010, and 89 percent of those children will be orphaned because of AIDS.

Although there appears to be no firm relationship between the HIV prevalence rate and the percentage of orphans from all causes—mainly because of the compounding nature of causes (AIDS, malaria, conflict, natural disaster, maternal death, and so forth)—one clear pattern emerges: the proportion of orphans arising from AIDS increases with the prevalence rate (figure 1.2). Countries/regions currently with a low prevalence of HIV can expect the proportion and number of AIDS orphans to increase in the near future as the prevalence rate rises.

The HIV/AIDS epidemic represents an unprecedented health, economic, and social threat that increases dramatically the nature and magnitude of people's risks and vulnerabilities. The pandemic is depleting entire communities of their most valuable resources, killing men and women in their most productive years and in their reproductive years. Besides depriving children of their basic needs and exposing them to extreme vulnerability, AIDS increases the risk that children will end up on the street, where they will be sexually abused or infected with HIV (Ramphele 2001) or caught up in criminal activities (Schoenteich 2001). AIDS undermines children's lives, and the fear of a "lost generation" is strong. If nothing is done, the risk of not meeting the Millennium Development Goals is high, and the prospect of future socioeconomic development will remain gloomy.

The challenges posed by the affected children and their families for all stakeholders and donors are enormous. Indeed, the long-term

Figure 1.2 HIV/AIDS Prevalence and Incidence of Orphans in Sub-Saharan Africa, 2001

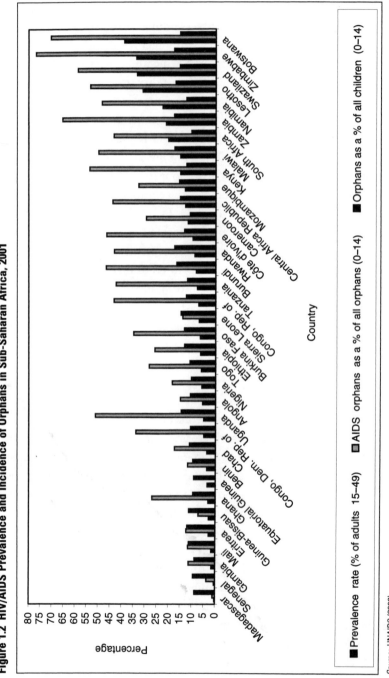

Source: UNAIDS (2002).

implications of the problem call for a search for solutions that can be sustained over the coming decades. A greater understanding of the impact of the epidemic on children is a prerequisite to better assessing their risks and needs and designing the appropriate programs to support them. The next chapter therefore seeks this understanding.

Notes

1. MAPs, which are described in appendix A, are currently the main instrument for channeling Bank assistance to orphans. AIDS refers to the acquired immunodeficiency syndrome; HIV refers to the human immunodeficiency virus.

2. For an elaboration of the concept of vulnerability in a social risk management framework, see Holzmann and Jorgensen (2000).

3. Moreover, as the epidemic evolves from low to high levels to a plateau, vulnerabilities will change.

4. Assets should be considered in broad terms—that is, as a wide range of tangible (land, labor, human and physical capital, savings) and intangible (social capital, network, proximity to markets, health and education facilities, empowerment) stores of values.

5. Unfortunately, the term *AIDS orphans* continues to be used among major stakeholders (governments, donors, local practitioners), because these children may face specific needs, and funds are often available for activities supporting affected and infected people. And so we use the term *AIDS orphans* in later parts of this study, but we certainly do not recommend the use of this term, which identifies orphans by the cause of death of their parents, in any operational activity focusing on orphans.

6. Some interventions, such as the development, enactment, and enforcement of OVC policies and legislation, or the abolition of school fees, may indeed help reach *all* orphans and other vulnerable children. Yet their implementation may prove difficult in some countries.

7. Unless otherwise indicated, the terms *orphans* and *OVC* are used interchangeably in the rest of this study.

8. Because orphans are more easily identified and thus numbered, they tend to receive much more attention than other vulnerable groups of children.

9. One must be cautious about these figures because they are based on epidemi-ological and demographic projections and therefore may not fully represent the reality. As *Children on the Brink 2002* states, "The methods used for *Children on the Brink 2002* were found to produce estimates of total orphan numbers that are in broad agreement (+/–20%) with survey-based estimates produced by the DHS [Demographic and Health Survey]. However, maternal and dual orphan numbers were consistently 40%–110% higher than those found by the DHS." Data from Rwanda illustrate this problem. Although the 1998–99 Multiple Indicator Cluster Survey (MICS) by the United Nations Children's Fund (UNICEF) found the incidence of orphanhood (double and single) to be 28.5 percent among children, the estimate by the Joint United Nations Programme on HIV/AIDS (UNAIDS) is only 17.5 percent, thereby downsizing the problem of orphanhood in Rwanda.

10. The prevalence of orphanhood depends not only on the magnitude of the epidemic, but also on its phase (Gregson, Garnett, and Anderson 1994).

CHAPTER 2

Understanding Orphans' Risks and Needs in Sub-Saharan Africa: The Demand Side

T he HIV/AIDS epidemic has placed, in severely hit regions, unbearable strains on families and communities by weakening their coping mechanisms and impoverishing them. Table 2.1 gives a sense of the damage AIDS can inflict on families, children, and communities. Relying on empirical research done in three countries (Ethiopia, Rwanda, and Uganda) of Sub-Saharan Africa, figure 2.1 summarizes the most important impacts of orphanhood on orphans themselves, communities, and the economy.

Children living in AIDS-affected areas, even though neither they nor their parents are infected with AIDS, are nevertheless exposed to increased vulnerabilities because they are "cared for by vulnerable families and reside in vulnerable communities" (Hunter and Williamson (1998b). The vulnerabilities, of course, increase greatly if the children live with parents infected with AIDS or if either parent or both parents are deceased. This chapter reviews the evidence bearing on the main risks and vulnerabilities faced by orphans, and it delineates a list of the major needs of orphans that should be met for them to develop normally.

The underlying concept adopted here has much more to do with risks, needs, and welfare than with rights, duties, and obligations, although we did not rely exclusively on the risk management framework, mainly because of lack of information and data constraints.[1]

Table 2.1 Potential Impacts of AIDS on Families, Children, and Communities

Potential impacts of AIDS on families	Potential impacts of AIDS on children	Potential impacts of AIDS on communities
– Loss of member, grief	– Loss of family and identity	– Reduced labor
– Impoverishment	– Depression	– Increased poverty
– Change in family composition and family and child roles	– Reduced well-being	– Inability to maintain infrastructure
– Forced migration	– Increased malnutrition, starvation	– Loss of skilled labor, including health workers and teachers
– Dissolution	– Failure to immunize or provide health care	– Reduced access to health care
– Stress	– Loss of health status	– Elevated morbidity and mortality
– Inability to give parental care to children	– Increased demand in labor	– Psychological stress and breakdown
– Loss of income for medical care and education	– Loss of school/educational opportunities	– Inability to marshal resources for community-wide funding schemes or insurance
– Demoralization	– Loss of inheritance	
– Long-term pathologies	– Forced migration	
– Increase in number of multigenerational households lacking middle generation	– Homelessness, vagrancy, crime	
	– Increased street living	
	– Exposure to HIV infection	

Source: Hunter and Williamson (1997), cited in UNAIDS (1999).

However, the approach adopted tends, like the human rights approach (HRA), to be child-centered and family- and community-focused. Unlike the HRA, which is guided by human rights, our approach is based on children's needs derived from the risks they face. Assessing children's risks and needs is an effective means of rapidly designing and implementing actions that will mitigate or eliminate these risks and that will ultimately promote realization of the human rights of the child. To this extent, the approach adopted in this study and the human rights approach are strongly complementary.

From table 2.1 it is possible to classify the major risks and vulnerabilities affecting orphaned children into two broad categories: (1) economic and social risks and vulnerabilities, and (2) psychological risks and vulnerabilities. Because of a lack of data disaggregated by gender, age group, and geographic area (such as urban or rural, low/high prevalence

Figure 2.1 Impacts of Parental Loss on Orphans, Sub-Saharan Africa

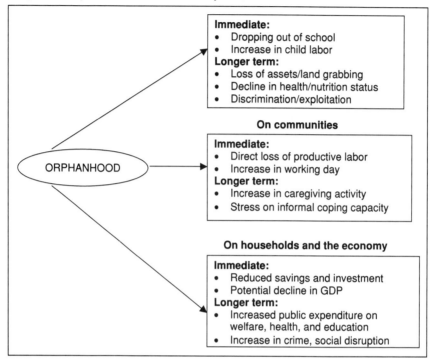

Source: Deininger, Garcia, and Subbarao (2003).

rate of HIV/AIDS), it is difficult to draw firm conclusions on the varied nature of risks faced by orphans and vulnerable children. However, where possible in this chapter, tentative patterns are presented.

Economic and Social Risks and Vulnerabilities

Orphanhood is often associated with increased economic and social risks and vulnerabilities. Poverty and consumption shortfalls, loss of human capital (including fewer school opportunities, health problems, and malnutrition), and exploitation and abuse are among the most common negative outcomes falling in this category. Each of these aspects is reviewed in this section.

Risk of Poverty and Consumption Shortfalls

Some attempts have been made to disentangle orphan status from poverty status, both for a cross-section of countries and for some individual countries. Data drawn from 10 countries suggest that orphans in Africa on average live in poorer households than nonorphans (Case, Paxson, and Ableidinger 2002). Indeed, the death of a father can have a disastrous impact on the welfare (wealth/income) of a household because of the costs of a funeral, the loss of income, and the risks of losing one's property (World Bank 1997, cited by Foster and Williamson 2000). Evidence also shows that orphans' care tends to fall more and more on the poorest homes—for example, those headed by the elderly or women.[2] Moreover, in some cases the death of one or both parents is followed by the dissolution of the family, leading to the integration of orphans into a new household, which makes the dependency ratio less favorable (Urassa and others 1997).[3] Unless foster families receive some kind of private transfers to cover the extra costs, resources per capita are likely to decrease.[4] A study based on a panel data set from Uganda showed that the addition of a foster child had the expected effects of not only reducing significantly the consumption and income per capita, but also reducing the capital accumulation of the household over the long term (Deininger, Garcia, and Subbarao 2003). Evidence from Rwanda also shows similar findings: the entry of an orphan induces a 21 percent decline in the estimated adult-equivalent per capita consumption (Siaens, Subbarao, and Wodon 2003).

Risk of Human Capital Erosion

Erosion of human capital is probably the biggest risk orphans and vulnerable children face in much of Africa. Exposure to multiple risks has critical impacts on school enrollments and the health and nutritional status of several million vulnerable children. The probability of not attaining the Millennium Development Goals is particularly high for children located in countries experiencing risk-compounding—that is, an orphan in a country emerging out of years of civil conflict and subjected to a severe covariate shock such as drought might face multiple risks and be very vulnerable to dropping out of school compared with another orphan placed in a country facing fewer overall challenges.

Fewer School Opportunities.   Faced with limited resources, foster house-holds might be expected to favor their biological children over foster ones,[5] and so deny orphans proper access to basic needs such as education, health care, and nutrition. For orphans living with their remaining parent, income shortfalls after the death of one parent may induce children to quit school. A study using data collected by the Demographic and Health Surveys and Living Standards Surveys for 22 countries in Sub-Saharan Africa in the 1990s shows much diversity in the relationship among orphan status, household wealth, and child school enrollment (Ainsworth and Filmer 2002).[6] The study notes that while there are some examples of large differentials in enrollment by orphan status, in the majority of cases the orphan enrollment gap is dwarfed by the gap between children from richer and poorer households. The authors conclude that the diverse find-ings demonstrate that the extent to which orphans are underenrolled rel-ative to other children is country-specific (e.g., a function of the national level of school enrollment or poverty level). Some country-specific studies do show the orphan disadvantage in school enrollment. This is the situa-tion in Rwanda (Siaens, Subbarao, and Wodon 2003—see figure 2.2) and in Tanzania, where Urassa and others (1997) observed that among children ages 13–17, orphans and foster children had significantly lower

Figure 2.2 School Enrollment Rates by Orphan Status and Age, Rwanda

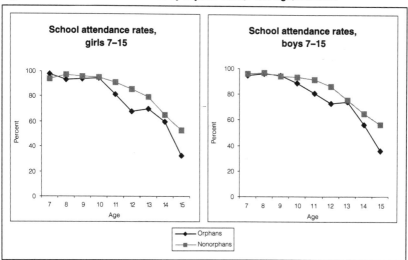

Source: Derived from equations reported in Siaens, Subbarao, and Wodon (2003).

school enrollment rates than children living with both parents. A similar conclusion was drawn by Case, Paxson, and Ableidinger (2002) based on data drawn from a cross-section of countries. Orphans of any type were less likely to be in school than the nonorphans with whom they lived. The largest effect was for double orphans, who were 10–30 percent less likely to go to school than the children with whom they lived. The authors also note that the schooling outcome is very much predicted by the degree of relatedness to the household head: the more distant the relationship of the household head to the orphan, the less likely it is that the orphan will be enrolled in school.

In Kampala, Uganda, 47 percent of households assisting orphans lacked money for education, compared with 10 percent of those households similarly placed but not charged with the responsibility for caring for orphans (Muller and Abbas 1990). Lack of money was a major problem mentioned by orphans in northern Uganda, especially among school-age orphans.

Further analysis is required, especially on school attendance and completion by gender and age groups. As for gender issues, evidence based on cross-country data suggests that, for school enrollment, female orphans are not disproportionately affected compared with male orphans (Ainsworth and Filmer 2002; Case, Paxson, and Ableidinger 2002). Country-specific studies, by contrast, show that female orphans are at a significant disadvantage. In Rwanda, for example, a much higher proportion of female orphans than boys are not in school (figure 2.2), and female orphans are also engaged in paid and unpaid work for much longer hours than boys (Siaens, Subbarao, and Wodon 2003—see figure 2.3).[7] As for variations by age group, the same study shows that the older the orphan, the greater is his or her risk of dropping out of school. Older orphans are more likely to be engaged in domestic work (including babysitting the younger children in the household) or in paid and unpaid productive activities.

The orphan disadvantage in school enrollment—to the extent it stems from financial hardship—could be greatly reduced, if not eliminated, if sectoral policies bearing on education were less restrictive (with no fees or uniforms) and more inclusive. After significant sectoral policy changes (such as the elimination of school fees and school uniforms) were implemented in Uganda between 1992 and 2002, Deininger, Garcia, and

Figure 2.3 Work Burden on Orphans and Nonorphans by Gender, Rwanda

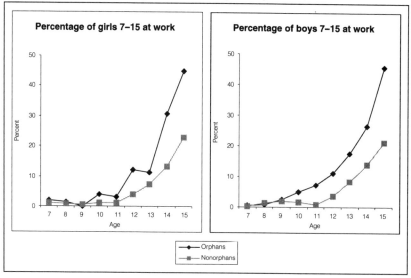

Source: Derived from equations reported in Siaens, Subbarao, and Wodon (2003).

Subbarao (2003) noted that the difference in school enrollment between foster and nonfoster children that existed in 1998 had disappeared by 2002. These findings suggest that in countries benefiting from the "Education for All" fast-track initiative, disparities in school enrollment among children may be substantially reduced.

Even when formal schooling outcomes are protected by pragmatic sectoral and household-specific policies, some unpreventable losses may still occur in the transfer of knowledge. The premature loss of parents may lead to a loss of intergenerational technical knowledge (such as better farming techniques) and parenting skills. It is hard to design policies to prevent such losses. One policy that may help to avoid such outcomes is to prolong the lives of HIV-positive parents as much as possible with appropriate medical treatment.

Health Risks of Orphanhood.   No clear pattern could be discerned about the health risks and the risk of malnutrition arising from orphanhood. Mortality risks did not differ among orphans, foster children, and children living with their parents in rural Tanzania (Urassa and others

1997), whereas in Uganda in 1999/2000 foster children were found to have significantly less access to health services than children living with their own parents (Deininger, Garcia, and Subbarao 2003). This situation has worsened over the years: in 1992 no discrimination against foster children was found, whereas in 2000 a lower percentage of foster children received immunization and vitamin A supplements (Deininger, Garcia, and Subbarao 2003). A study in Rakai, Uganda, revealed that some young orphans were stunted and malnourished because of the inability of the extended family to cope with the increasing number of orphans (Barnett and Blaikie 1992, cited by Ntozi and others 1999). Stunting among orphaned children was also observed in the Kagera region in Tanzania (Ainsworth and Semali 2000). In Sierra Leone, foster girls seemed particularly vulnerable to malnutrition (Bledsoe, Ewbank, and Isiugo-Abanihe 1988). A similar finding was observed in Burundi, where 24 percent of female orphans suffered from severe malnutrition (severe wasting) compared with 14 percent of male orphans and 12.5 percent of nonorphans. More striking was the impact of the death of the mother on stunting and wasting outcomes (ISTEEBU 2001).[8]

Risk of Exploitation and Abuse

Children living with sick parents are often already engaged in the household's economic activity. Some evidence suggests that the children's workload increases once their parents die, and especially that of those children who become head of the household. Because most of the latter children lack the required skills or inputs to conduct household economic activities, households headed by a child or adolescent are often found in dire straits. For those orphans living with foster families, there is some evidence that their workload is greater than that of the nonorphans living in the same household (Foster and others 1997b, cited by Foster and Williamson 2000). In Burundi, data based on the last multisectoral cluster survey reveal that although 24 percent of male nonorphans and 27 percent of female nonorphans work more than four hours a day, the proportion increases to 36 percent for male orphans and 40.5 percent for female orphans (ISTEEBU 2001). The proportion of female orphans working more than four hours a day is particularly high when the mother has died (52 percent), suggesting that girls tend to cover some of their late mother's tasks within the household. Higher work burdens were also observed in Rwanda among female orphans fostered in urban households (Siaens, Subbarao, and Wodon 2003). However, because child labor in Africa relies mainly on family-based activities, lack of access to assets such as land or livestock after the death of parents may force the poorest orphans into idleness (Andvig 2001).

Orphaned children may also be exposed to mistreatment by their foster family. Risks of abuse, neglect, and exploitation are often reported (Ntozi and others 1999, for northern Uganda; Mann 2002, for Malawi) and seem to increase with age. Teenage female orphans seem particularly at risk of being put to work at intensive household chores because of cultural practices and the limited educational opportunities available to them, and of being physically and sexually abused. Indeed, the lack of parental protection and supervision may leave a door open to violation of rights, such as those just mentioned, and property grabbing. A study by the Ministry of Health of Kenya showed that many orphans, especially boys living with their single mothers, were denied property rights (Chipfakacha 2002). Similarly, in Uganda it was found that widows and orphans were often subjected to property snatching and loss of inheritance (Wakhweya 2003). Evidence from South Africa and Namibia suggests that in some extreme cases, orphans who live on the streets are exposed to prostitution, drug abuse, HIV infection, and crime (Webb 1995, cited by Ntozi and others 1999).

Psychological Risks and Associated Vulnerabilities

Psychological aspects have often been overlooked in the literature, in part because of the difficulty in assessing trauma and its impacts.[9] Indeed, psychological impacts are often not visible, they take different forms, and they may not arise until months after the traumatic event (HUMULIZA/Terre des Hommes Switzerland 1999). The death of a parent leaves children in a state of trauma. Sengendo and Nambi reported in 1997 that in Uganda many orphans were showing signs of stress and trauma (Sengendo and Nambi 1997, cited by Foster and Williamson 2000). Indeed, orphans may become withdrawn and passive or develop

Table 2.2 Summary of Common Trauma Reactions by Age: War-Affected Children, Refugee Camps, Cambodia, 1990

Trauma reaction	Preschool	School age	Adolescent
Fears, worries		✓	✓
Physical complaints		✓	✓
Attention, memory problems			✓
Nightmares, sleep problems			✓
Post-traumatic play	✓	✓	
Regression, separation, anxiety	✓	✓	
Anger, hostility, depression		✓	✓
Apathy, withdrawal, avoidance		✓	✓
Sadness/depression		✓	✓
Sense of foreshortened future		✓	✓
Survivor guilt			✓
Risky, dangerous behavior			✓

Source: Mollica (2003).

sadness, anger, fear, and antisocial behaviors and become violent or depressed. Table 2.2, which is reproduced from a study by Mollica (2003), summarizes the trauma reactions experienced by war-affected children living in refugee camps in Cambodia. The data were drawn from a study conducted in two refugee camps in Cambodia in 1990. Although the causes of the trauma were different, similar reactions were observed among children who had lost a parent (HUMULIZA/Terre des Hommes Switzerland 1999: 42–5).

Orphans may experience additional trauma from lack of nurturance, guidance, and a sense of attachment, which may impede their socialization process (through damaged self-confidence, social competencies, motivation, and so forth). Children often find it difficult to express their fear, grievance, and anger effectively. In addition, when willing to express their feelings, they may find it difficult to find a sensitive ear (UNAIDS 2001). Evidence has shown that sick parents are often not able to talk about their disease with their children for fear of causing distress. Yet, by not including the child in their confidence, parents do indeed cause more distress (HUMULIZA/Terre des Hommes Switzerland 1999; Poulter 1997). Moreover, adults (such as surviving and foster parents, teachers)—when not themselves suffering from some forms of trauma or depression and thus unable to deal with the child's emotional needs—are rarely aware of children's emotional and psychological needs. Finally, children's behavioral changes may not be always understood as distress, and may sometimes be punished by the adult or just ignored.

When a parent dies from AIDS, trauma is often accompanied by stigma and discrimination. At school, AIDS orphans may be singled out or rejected by their schoolmates, which can create barriers to health care, education, and access to social events.[10] In the study conducted in Nshamba and Kagera, Tanzania, all orphans interviewed reported harassment by schoolmates and peers (HUMULIZA/Terre des Hommes Switzerland 1999). Similar findings were reported in Malawi, where some orphans described having stones thrown at them, being insulted, or having less access, among other things, to food, material items, and school opportunities than the other children in the household (Mann 2002). Those children infected by HIV/AIDS experience additional anxiety and fear. Evidence from Ethiopia shows that one of the major concerns of HIV/AIDS-infected children is the fear of being forgotten once they die (SC-USA 2001). AIDS orphans or HIV-positive children may face extreme discrimination that leads to isolation and risky behaviors and dropping out of school.

What Are the Specific Needs of Orphans?

Effective interventions depend on knowing the specific needs of orphans. These needs, which can be derived directly from the vulnerabilities and risks just delineated, are presented in table 2.3.

Such needs, however, should be adapted to fit in with age- and gender-specific risks and vulnerabilities (see appendix B, table B.2). But the data required to come up with strong conclusions are often missing, and so additional research is needed. For example, it would be of particular interest to know more about the treatment of female orphans, because there is evidence that girls in impoverished and uprooted situations are most vulnerable in terms of their labor, nutrition and health, and abuse. Field experience suggests that often female orphans are fostered not so much for their protection or welfare, but largely so that they can provide

Table 2.3 Children's Risks/Vulnerabilities and Needs

Risks/vulnerabilities	Needs
Reduced economic resources of the family, housing	Adequate productive skills; access to income-generating activities, to productive inputs
Risk (loss) of educational opportunities	Uninterrupted access to education; may need fee waivers, subsidies, training in skills—sector policy issue
Malnutrition and lack of adequate health care	Adequate nutrition and access to health care—sector policy issue
Property grabbing	Social and legal protection
Abuse, exploitation, discrimination	Social and legal protection
Psychological trauma, conflict stigmatization	Psychosocial support; loving and caring environment

Source: The authors.

temporary support for the chores of an extended family, or of families headed by females (Siaens, Subbarao, and Wodon 2003).

Similarly, the nature of vulnerabilities and needs varies by age: children under 5 might face greater risk of malnutrition, whereas children between 7 and 14 years of age might be more at the risk of dropping out of school and prone to abuses. A recently published guideline for early childhood development has addressed the issue of orphans under age 5 (Young 2002; also see World Bank 2003b). The problems facing older children (adolescents) have generally been overlooked, not only within the issues pertaining to orphanhood, but more generally within the issues related to health and skills training. The proportion of adolescent orphans to total number of orphans appears very high in most countries, which suggests the need to address the issues surrounding adolescents more thoroughly than in the past. In northern Uganda, for example, the percentage of AIDS orphans rises from 24.4 percent for the infancy and 0–1 age group to 40 percent for the 10–14 age group, but falls to 38 percent for the 15–17 age group (Ntozi and others 1999). In Tanzania, the proportion of orphaned children from all causes also rose rapidly with age: from 3 percent for those under 5 years of age, to 18 percent for those 15–17 years of age (Urassa and others 1997). The main reason for this tendency is that AIDS kills parents in midlife after an incubation period of 8–10 years. The chance of being an orphan therefore increases with

Table 2.4 Risks Faced by Orphans, by Age Group

Infant	Pre-school-age children	School-age children	Adolescent
– Exposure to HIV/AIDS (mother-child transmission through breastfeeding and birth)	– Loss of social contact and stimulation	– Becoming caretakers for parents and siblings	– Further increase in responsibilities as provider and caretaker
– Frequent infections	– Begin to experience and respond to the trauma of loss (parents, siblings, home)	– Losing access to education	– Exclusion from education
– Poor nutrition	– Poor nutrition and growth	– Increasing awareness of stigma	– Poor self-esteem
– Poor growth	– Exposure to abusive environments	– Sexual abuse	– Depression
– Emotional deprivation	– Decreasing role of frequent infections	– Physical and verbal abuse	– Sexual abuse/teen pregnancy
– Developmental delays		– Depression	– Sexually transmitted illnesses, including HIV
– Attachment disorders		– Increasing workload (child labor)	– Exclusion from formal employment

Sources: Robbins (2003); Makhweya (2003).

the child's age. Table 2.4 summarizes the different risks faced by orphans according to their age group.

Notes

1. See appendix C for an overview of the child's right approach, and Holzmann and Jorgensen (2000) and Heitzmann, Canagarajah, and Siegel (2002) for an overview of the social risk management framework.

2. A new pattern is emerging for caregivers: the maternal kin are becoming the main caregiver, whereas in the past caregiving was the responsibility of the paternal extended family (Urassa and others 1997; Case, Paxson, and Ableidinger 2002). Chapter 3 presents a more detailed analysis of the caregivers. In Rwanda, orphans tend to be found in relatively better-off households (Siaens, Subbarao, and Wodon 2003).

3. The dependency ratio is defined as the sum of children under 18 and persons 60 years or older divided by the number of persons between 18 and 59 years of age.

4. Private transfers of assets within families have for a long time been considered a major informal mechanism of distress alleviation. However, this mechanism seems to have weakened because of the HIV/AIDS crisis. In Tanzania,

less than 10 percent of orphans received some material support from outside relatives (Urassa and others 1997).

5. As Case, Paxson, and Ableidinger (2002) appropriately write, "Adults may be willing to invest more in their own children, both because their affinity to their own children is greater, and because they are more likely to receive transfers from their children later in life."

6. Most studies focus on school enrollment. Little is known about school attainment and attendance among orphans and nonorphans.

7. Figures 2.2 and 2.3 are derived from equations estimated and reported in Siaens, Subbarao and Wodon (2003) using the Integrated Household Living Conditions Survey, Rwanda, conducted during 1999–2001.

8. Stunting refers to a low height for age because of chronic malnutrition, and wasting refers to a low weight for height as a result of acute malnutrition.

9. Most of the literature concerns the psychosocial needs related to conflict. Yet, even though the traumatic events experienced differ substantially, the psychological symptoms shown are quite similar. Therefore, the points made in the following section remain valid for most types of orphans and vulnerable children who have experienced traumatic events.

10. Exclusion from school, by breaking up a child's routine and isolating him or her even more from social life situations, is a major factor in increasing an orphan's psychosocial disorder (HUMULIZA/Terre des Hommes Switzerland 1999).

CHAPTER 3

The Supply Side: Caregivers and Their Strengths and Weaknesses

C hapter 2 identified the problem of orphans and other vulnerable children (OVC) from the "demand side"—that is, who needs care, and what are the needs of OVC. This chapter turns to the "supply side"—that is, who are the caregivers, what are their strengths and weaknesses, and how should their capacity to provide for the care of orphans be assessed.

Caregivers can be classified into two broad categories: household-based care and institutional care.[1] Household-based care is provided by a living parent, the extended family, a household headed by a child or adolescent, or nonrelatives (foster care or adoption). Institutional care is provided by a foster home or surrogate family groups integrated in a community; a children's village; or an orphanage.

Household-Based Care

Household-based care is the dominant form of caring arrangement for orphaned children throughout Africa, and for most stakeholders it remains the most desired model of care for these children. In line with traditional practices, the integration of orphans within their close relatives is given priority. Yet, when such integration is not possible, adoption and formal fostering are given consideration, too, although they do not yet appeal to the public because of cultural bias.

Living within Family Lines

Throughout Sub-Saharan Africa, fostering[2] within family lines remains the most common safety net for the care of orphans. In rural Tanzania, 95 percent of the orphans are taken care of by relatives. A similar pattern was found in Uganda and Zambia (see table 3.1). This practice, deeply embedded in the African culture, has, without a doubt, favored the smooth absorption of the growing number of orphans despite noticeable changes, such as the increased involvement of the maternal relatives (Urassa and others 1997; Case, Paxson, and Ableidinger 2002), elders (grandparents), and the young (Beers and others 1996, cited by Hunter and Williamson 2000; Foster and others 1996; Foster and others 1997a). Another important feature is the changing nature of fosterage from "voluntary" to a "necessity" (Aspaas 1999). "Crisis fosterage" implies that more and more orphans are being "pushed" into households rather

Table 3.1 Who Is Caring for Orphans: Uganda, Zambia, and Tanzania

Country	Sample covered	Caregiver (percent)
Northern Uganda	Districts of Arua, Soroti, and Lira (1997) 2,119 orphans	Surviving parent (43) Uncle and aunt (16) Grandparents (22) Older orphans (19) Other relatives (3)
Zambia	National survey (1996)	Grandparents (38) Extended family (55) Older orphans (11) Nonrelatives (6)
Uganda	Luweero District 732 orphans	Grandparents (32) Surviving parent (50) Extended family (16) Nonrelatives (5)
Rural Tanzania	Mawezi Regional Hospital 297 orphans	Grandparents (43) Surviving parent (27) Extended family (15) Older orphans (10) Community (5)

Sources: Northern Uganda: Ntozi and others (1999); Zambia: Government of Zambia (1999), as cited in Deininger, Garcia, and Subbarao (2003); Uganda: Monk (2001), as cited in Deininger, Garcia, and Subbarao (2003); rural Tanzania: Lusk, Huffman, and O'Gara (2000), as cited in Deininger, Garcia, and Subbarao (2003).
Note: Most data come from household surveys, and therefore do not address adequately the problem of OVC in the streets and in residential care.

than being pulled, making them vulnerable (Castle 1995, cited by Aspaas 1999).[3]

By staying with known relatives and other children, orphans may grow up in a more stable and secure environment favoring their psychological, intellectual, and social development. However, when resources are allocated to meet basic needs (e.g., food, education, or clothing), they may suffer from discrimination. Foster parents may favor their biological children first either because of the resource dilution effect (i.e., the decrease in per capita household resources after orphans enter the household) or because of other reasons. Research has shown that the difference in the school attendance of orphans and of nonorphans is explained mostly by the greater tendency of orphans to live with distant relatives or unrelated caregivers (Case, Paxson, and Ableidinger 2002). Care provided by aunts, uncles, and other relatives may be adequate if the caregiver has the economic means needed to support the additional members of the household and is motivated to provide adequate care. Yet it cannot be assumed that orphans in better-off households are necessarily better off.

Developing the appropriate mechanisms to ensure that children are well treated is becoming important. Communities, together with local authorities, whether traditional or faith-based, are more likely to successfully supervise fostering and prevent and counter child abuse than staff members of ministries of social affairs. Indeed, ministries of social affairs in Sub-Saharan Africa are poorly staffed most of the time, and the workers they do have are often badly paid and unmotivated to make rural visits. In addition, their actions in the field may be limited. Indeed, what happens within a household is more visible to neighbors, communities, and visitors from local associations, or to traditional and faith-based authorities. Therefore, it is unlikely that social workers effectively uncover abuses of fostered children within households; peer and community pressure seem to be much more reliable in this area. The role of communities in the design of appropriate care strategies for orphans is further discussed in chapter 6.

Living with the Surviving Parent.   Although the surviving parent is usually the principal caregiver, single orphans do not always remain with their living parent. Often the death of one parent, especially the mother, is followed by the dissolution of the family. This practice is quite common throughout Africa, and it increased significantly for maternal orphans during the last decade. In 2000 in Malawi, 73 percent of maternal orphans and 29 percent of paternal orphans were not living with their surviving parents. In 1992 these percentages were 48 percent and 27 percent, respectively, and similar patterns can be observed in Ghana, Kenya, and Tanzania (Case, Paxson, and Ableidinger 2002). Fathers may find it more and more difficult to care for their children and prefer sending them to relatives. Remarriage, migration, and disease also may account for the family dislocation.

Living with the surviving parent, when feasible, ensures that siblings remain together in a familiar environment. However, the death of one parent may entail a significant drop in the family welfare. With the death of the main breadwinner (often the father), economic needs are very likely not to be met, and basic needs (e.g., adequate food, health care, nutrition, schooling, shelter) may become difficult to provide as the revenue of the family drops. Meanwhile, the workload of children may increase, and paternal orphans may be subject to expropriation when relatives claim a right to the widow's or the orphan's property. In addition, evidence suggests that most orphans do not receive adequate psychological support. The surviving parents may face enormous difficulties in meeting the needs of their children, especially if the parents are themselves sick. For orphans who are likely to lose their surviving parent (especially from HIV/AIDS), alternative support should be designed well before the surviving parent dies.[4]

Caregiving by the Extended Family.   Single orphans who are not taken care of by their surviving parent and double orphans are usually absorbed by their extended families. With the rapid spread of the HIV/AIDS epidemic, however, some changes are taking place. Uncles and aunts, the traditional first choice as substitute caregivers, are less available—either because they are themselves victims of AIDS or because they are now more reluctant to foster orphans (and usually more than one so that orphan siblings are not separated).[5] Therefore, grandparents and older orphans are forced to take on this new role (Foster and others 1996; Krift and Phiri 1998). In many settings, grandparents appear to be the most common caregivers. In northern Uganda in 1997, 22 percent of orphans were taken care of by their grandparents, while in rural Tanzania, the proportion was 43 percent (see table 3.1).

Although grandparents may provide a secure and loving environment that helps children to socialize, they may find it difficult to respond to children's psychological, legal, economic, and basic needs. Grandparents may be old, and they may be themselves sick and tired. They usually face strong material constraints and receive little external support.[6] External support may help, but this type of care can be difficult to sustain over the long run because the current generation of grandparents will die. It is therefore important in these situations that some kind of alternative support be arranged before the grandparents' death so that the orphans do not have to be sent from one home to another.

A non-negligible proportion of orphaned children are under the care of older orphans. This situation has emerged in 7–10 percent of cases in rural Tanzania and almost 20 percent of cases in northern Uganda (Ntozi and others 1999). Although the latter figure is quite high and does not represent the general situation, child-headed families are becoming more and more visible.[7] A survey conducted of 43 orphan heads of household in Manicaland, Zimbabwe, helps to illuminate the reasons for the establishment of such households (Foster and others 1997a). The most frequent reasons given were: (a) no known relative in the family was able to take care of the children; (b) the relatives did not want to take care of the children (because they had their own lives to live, they had no space, they were in need of care themselves, or they had no love for the children); (c) the children did not want to move to the relative's household (especially if the relatives were living close by and would visit them regularly). Evidence also suggests that one important motivation for the formation of child-headed households is the desire not to split up the siblings and to retain access to, and ownership of, the family's land and other property.

By avoiding being split up among various relatives and being able to stay in their home in familiar surroundings, children may face less emotional and psychological trauma. However, this situation puts the child or adolescent head in a role that he or she may not be prepared to undertake, even if visited regularly by close relatives or friends.[8] The lack of money may cause orphans to drop out of school and to work excessively for little reward. The lack of productive skills to run the parent's occupation, or the seizure of the land may also force the child-headed household into deeper poverty and may increase the risks of being pressed onto the street with all its attendant adverse consequences. Such households are very vulnerable, and unlikely to meet all their needs. Child- and adolescent-headed households will clearly need special attention and support. However, such support must be carefully designed to avoid any adverse side-effects. Luzze has observed that in Uganda "careless interventions by NGOs have destroyed the community social support systems of orphans and actually contributed to the proliferation of child-headed families."[9]

The emergence of the child-headed household has sometimes been perceived as a sign that the extended family system has reached a saturation point. There is no doubt that the rapid spread of the AIDS pandemic casts some doubts on the ability of the extended family to absorb more and more orphans and provide them with adequate care in the near future. Alternative types of care are needed for some children. Foster care and adoption are two forms of care, among others, that provide a family-like setting for orphans who do not have any relatives to foster them.

Living with Unrelated Families

Fostering and adoption by nonrelatives are not very common throughout Sub-Saharan Africa.[10] The deeply rooted tradition of child fostering within the extended family may be one of the main reasons for the slow development of adoption in much of Africa. In some contexts, taboos and cultural beliefs also may discourage people from taking unrelated children into their home. In Zimbabwe, the fear of invoking *ngozi* (the avenging spirit) is strong (Parry 1998). In South Africa, obstacles such as tribal allegiances and animism mitigate against adoption. Some anecdotal evidence suggests that in specific contexts fostering and adoption by unrelated families have increased without any external support. For example, after the 1994 genocide in Rwanda many families fostered unrelated children. The fostering was perceived to be a moral imperative because so many children were orphaned.

Fostering with unrelated families may be undertaken formally (legal binds are required) or informally (children are not committed by court order). In formal fostering, child placement follows a legal process in which a social worker is in charge of identifying a suitable foster parent or parents for the child; placement is under the supervision of the welfare bureau.[11] In general, foster parents are entitled to a monthly support allowance—sometimes until the child reaches legal maturity (18 years old)—to help them cover some of the expenses incurred in raising the child. Yet very low-income countries such as Malawi are finding it difficult to provide such support. Despite the fact that some foster parents have complained about delays in receipt of the material support to which they are entitled, it appears that, globally, parents who have formally fostered or adopted orphans are not really relying on this aid (Bandawe and Louw 1997). Informal fostering with or without alien parents also tends to face the same constraints in public support.

Another aspect of placement practices is authority and bonding. Formal fostering and adoption implies that the foster or adoptive family will take full responsibility for the child and is authorized to make all decisions related to the child. By contrast, in informal fosterage there is no statutory supervision or accountability, because no legal guardian has been appointed. This situation raises some legal issues about the child's rights.[12] Unlike informally fostered children, formally fostered and adopted children become full members of the family and share the same rights as the biological children, including inheritance. Formal fostering also entails strong bonding between the child and his or her foster family. However, the relationship may be broken at any time by the social worker (e.g., upon presentation of evidence of child abuse or of a child's maladjustment to his or her new family).

In all types of placement, *the child's protection is a major concern.* Because the child is desired—parents who formally foster or adopt orphans do so of their own will—one would expect orphans to be well treated and given good opportunities to develop themselves physically, emotionally, and socially. In addition, because foster and adoptive parents unrelated to the children are often (self-)selected, they should have the economic means[13] to meet the basic needs of their children. Ideally, any placed child should be visited regularly by a social worker to ensure that he or she is adapting well to the new environment. Yet supervision visits by employees of the welfare bureaus are often hampered by insufficient means (such as lack of adequate transport) and human resources (too few social workers, often overwhelmed).[14] In Kenya, although children's officers are expected to visit fostered children at least once every two months, evidence reveals that, in practice, supervision visits are quite rare, sometimes less than once every two years (Adhiambo Ogwang 2001). In addition, lack of adequate training, as well as lack of referral to a temporary place of safety and effective sanctions in cases of abuse, strongly limit the scope of the role played by social workers. Peer and community pressure seems in many cases to be a more relevant and cost-effective option.

Increased fosterage and adoption by nonrelatives, if properly practiced, are an effective alternative in child care. Yet they will require important changes, such as a shift in people's attitudes and a better adjustment of legal practices to the African cultural context.[15] In South Africa, potential caregivers prefer informal fostering[16] arrangements (Parry 1998). Moreover, "a broadening of current definitions of parenthood and parenting and a reappraisal of the qualities regarded as desirable in prospective adoptive parents" is required (Brink 1998). In Kenya, prospective parents are found among couples, but also among single women at least 21 years of age. Whether to expand this right to single males above age 21 is under consideration (Adhiambo Ogwang 2001). However, as urbanization progresses and traditional beliefs wane, and as the number of orphans increases, obstacles to fostering and adoption by unrelated families will certainly weaken. Yet some countries such as Eritrea have formally forbidden fosterage within alien families.

The issue of economic support—a major hindrance to formal fostering and adoption—also would have to be reviewed. Some governments (e.g., in Botswana, Malawi, Rwanda, South Africa, and Uganda) have already taken some actions in that direction such as providing material support and monthly allowances. Research in Zimbabwe has shown that when some support is given, families are willing to foster unrelated children. However, in Rwanda some abuses were observed (e.g., increased child labor and fewer school opportunities for double orphans fostered in unrelated families) among foster families receiving some cash support.[17] In any case, the establishment of effective fostering and adoption services, with effective supervision mechanisms, is a prerequisite for the sound development of such models of child care. Strengthening the capacity of social workers to conduct their work adequately would be desirable.

As the number of orphans grows, finding appropriate foster parents is very time-consuming, and a move toward favoring wider institutional placements may become the only pragmatic solution in some countries. Institutionalization also may be a solution for orphans who have no one to care for them, especially those with special needs such as handicapped or HIV-positive children.

Institutional Care

In Africa, institutional care for orphans is quite limited; according to MacLeod (2001), only 1–3 percent of orphans are cared for in institutional settings (and up to 5 percent in some specific zones). Yet all children in institutions are not orphans. Evidence from Ethiopia, Tanzania, and Uganda clearly demonstrates that fact. With the sharp increase in orphans in Africa and the process of deinstitutionalization, new and innovative forms of institutional or semi-institutional care have emerged, such as children's homes and children's villages. But these forms vary widely in size, management, and effectiveness.

Statutory Residential Care

Statutory residential care refers to the accommodation of orphans in institutions removed from their community (MacLeod 2001). This form of care may be appropriate for orphans with no one to take care of them and those with special needs such as orphans who are HIV-positive or who are handicapped. A growing number of facilities are looking after HIV/AIDS orphans, and some of them are providing infected children with palliative care and psychological support. The costs associated with such care often limit the number of children who can be treated.

Orphanages are by far the most formal type of institutions that care for orphans. Most orphanages are run by nongovernmental organizations (NGOs), religious organizations (with grants from governments and donors), or governments. In this setting, orphans are cared for by social workers, and their basic needs such as shelter, food, clothing, and education are met. Orphanages are often believed to provide children with adequate basic care, although much depends on the quality of that care. Interaction between the community and the orphanage is not very common, especially when children are sent to the orphanage's school rather than to the public school.

Major drawbacks are said to be associated with orphanages, but few have been studied. Ethiopia's orphanages are well documented, however. Chernet (2001) provides an extensive list of problems associated with institutional care in Ethiopia:

- Inadequate funding

- Shortage of trained personnel

- Inadequate skills

- Lack of psychosocial services

- Lack of long-term strategic planning

- Feeling of loneliness and helplessness on the part of orphans

- Dependency

- Low self-esteem

- Lack of adult guidance

- Limited participation of children in decisions about their future.

Family-Like Setting

In recognition of the adverse impacts of residential care on the development of children, a growing number of countries (such as Eritrea, Ethiopia, and Uganda) have begun to deinstitutionalize orphanages and rely on alternative forms of institutional arrangements that tend to re-create a family-like setting. Children's group homes and children's villages are the most popular forms developed.

Children's Homes.   A *children's home* is an arrangement in which a paid and usually trained foster mother lives with a group of orphans (generally from 4 to 10 children) in an ordinary home (rather than an institutional building) within the community. Children's homes are usually supported by NGOs or private sponsors, and they may or may not be registered. When they are not registered, supervision and monitoring of the children's well-being are not legally required unless the children have been placed in the home by the court. These homes sometimes serve as temporary "holding places" for children who are waiting for a permanent placement within a foster family.

By providing children with a family-like setting and a trained mother, these homes should adequately meet orphans' basic material, safety, and psychological needs. However, lack of a father figure may be a problem, especially for the socialization of male orphans.

The sustainability of this type of care depends to a large extent on the monitoring supervision and support of social workers and the level of external financing. By allowing children to evolve in their own community, well-organized children's homes may offer a viable option in communities heavily affected by the orphan crisis and where women are heavily overburdened with the care of both orphans and sick adults.

Children's Villages.   Different concepts of the *children's village* have emerged in the recent past. The concept developed by SOS Children's Village usually consists of a group of about 10–20 houses, which form a community and provide a family-like setting for vulnerable children. Each house is headed by an SOS-trained mother, who takes care of 8–10 children. Children grow up in conditions comparable to those in "normal families" in the sense that biological siblings are not split up, children of different ages and gender become brothers and sisters, all children are enrolled in public schools, and all children are strongly encouraged to maintain contacts with the community. The village director (a male) supports the mothers and represents a father figure to the children. SOS Children's Villages are sponsored by an NGO, and as such they are not self-sustaining. These villages have often been criticized for separating children from the community and for providing a standard of material well-being so much higher than that of the surrounding community that it causes the children significant difficulties with social reintegration once they leave the village.

Some variations on this type of care have been developed within the framework of the deinstitutionalization of care[18] being undertaken in some countries such as Ethiopia and Uganda. Formal orphanages are transformed into community-based resources centers where day care services for foster parents and skill training programs for older children are made available (UNAIDS 2002).

A children's village seems to meet most of orphans' basic and economic needs; uncertainties remain, however, about whether psychological and safety needs are met. Such villages can thrive only as long as (a) resources are available; (b) children are raised in an environment not too different from their original one; (c) children are part of the life of the neighborhood community;[19] (d) trained social workers are available for monitoring and supervision; and (e) the neighborhood community shares a part of the cost of running the village.[20] Not surprisingly, there are only very few examples of such well-functioning children's villages.

Care of Orphans: Assessing Community Capacity and Responses

The magnitude of the orphan crisis means that policymakers must consider all forms of acceptable caring responses by communities. Evidence suggests that 95 percent of orphans are indeed taken care of within families and communities. Nevertheless, the experience reviewed in this chapter also suggests that the extended family and communities are sometimes being stretched to the point to which orphans' welfare may be threatened. How does one determine exactly when a community has

Table 3.2 Indicators and Information Sources to Help Assess Weakening or Saturation of Extended Family Safety Net within a Community

Indicator	Sources of information
Proportion of orphans fostered in households headed by elderly caregivers	Registration of children by the community
Proportion of child-headed households	Household surveys such as the Multiple Indicator Cluster Survey (MICS), Living Standards Measurement Survey (LSMS), and census
Proportion of households with orphans from two or more families (sibling dispersal)	
Proportion of orphaned street children	

Sources: The authors, based on Halkett (1998) and Foster and Williamson (2000).

reached its limits to provide care? Is there an objective way in which one can assess a community's caring capacity and determine what support it might require to continue providing care?

Tables 3.2 and 3.3 list community and household vulnerability indices. Table 3.2 presents some indicators of a weakening of the extended family as a safety net for orphans' care. If the percentages of the indicators listed in this table are high and increasing, the extended family in that community has reached a saturation point.

The indicators in table 3.3 can be computed to produce a score useful in evaluating the ability of households to cope. The final score is obtained by summing up the values of the subscores calculated. *The larger the final*

Table 3.3 Capacity to Cope at the Household Level

Indicator	Subscore
DEMOGRAPHIC CHARACTERISTICS – *Who is the household head?*	If the head is a(an): adult male: 0 adult female: 1 elderly: 2 child: 3
– Number of adults (18–59 years) – Number of elderly (60 years and older) – *Number* of children: biological/*fostered/orphans* →*Dependency ratio: adults/(children + elderly)*	Number of fostered children/orphans 1/ ratio value
ECONOMIC CHARACTERISTICS *Housing:* – Housing condition (roof and walls)[a] – Number of rooms (excluded kitchen) →*Occupation rate: number of persons/room* *(i.e., household size/number of rooms)*	 Index value: between 0 and 4 Index value: between 0 and 4 *Value of the occupation rate*
Wealth: – If household possesses: house radio arable land[b] livestock[b] private business[c] – If household receives remittances[b] – If household has another income-generating activity – If the household head or spouse has a formal job – If the household has been expropriated (property grabbing)	 Yes: 0, no: 2 Yes: 0, no: 2 Yes: 0, no: 2 Yes: 0, no: 2 Yes: 0, no: 2 Yes: 0, no: 2 Yes: 0, no: 2 Yes: 0 , no: 2 Yes: 2 , no: 0

(Continued)

(Continued from p. 37)

COPING MECHANISMS: COMPARING BIOLOGICAL CHILDREN'S AND FOSTERED/ORPHANED CHILDREN'S SCHOOL PARTICIPATION AND WORK LOAD	
Primary school enrollment	If all children are benefiting: 0
	If equal among all children: 0
	If none: 2
	If biological > orphans: 3
	If biological < orphans: 1
Comparison of children's workload (hours per week)	If equal: 0
	If biological > orphans: 1
	If biological < orphans: 3
(Comparisons should be made within similar gender and age groups.)	
Number of sick persons living in the family (long-lasting disease)	Number of sick persons
If guardian is sick (long-lasting disease)	Yes: 2, no: 0
FINAL SCORE: added values	
MAIN SOURCE OF DATA: household surveys, home visits	

Source: The authors.

[a] For the roof, the evaluator could distinguish between (4) straw, (3) stubble or wood, (2) unburned brick (adobe), (1) burned brick, and (0) cement. For the walls, the evaluator could distinguish between (4) straw, (3) unburned brick (adobe), (2) wood, (1) sheet iron, and (0) tile or cement.

[b] When possible, the evaluator could be more precise and ask for the number of hectares of arable land possessed, the number of livestock (cattle, small stock) possessed, and the amount of remittance received. From this additional information, the evaluator could create new bounds based on quartile and compute more accurate subscores: 3: low, 2: average, 1: good, 0: very good. For example, suppose that 25 percent of households in the sample own 4 head of cattle or less, 25 percent between 5 and 10 head, 25 percent between 11 and 20 head, and the 25 percent remaining more than 20 head of cattle. For a household belonging to the first quartile, the subscore would be 3.

score, the worse is the coping situation within the household. To be useful, such score must allow assessment of the capacity of different households to take care of orphans and other vulnerable children. This can be achieved by computing a mean or median score according to various household characteristics such as (a) the type of household head (female, male, elderly, or child; (b) the number of fostered children in the household; and (c) the presence or absence of sick persons in the household. Some indicators presented in table 3.3 may be too broad to be really relevant. Yet, when possible, the indicators should be disaggregated (as indicated in notes a and b to the table). A practical example of how to compute such an indicator is provided in the appendix D to this volume.

Clearly, any scoring method will necessarily contain some elements of arbitrariness. This scoring method gives at best a static, one-shot picture.

But experience suggests that the temporal dimension is important; orphans may be passed from one caregiver to another because no one situation is stable or sustainable over time. One way to supplement the score-driven quantitative approach is use of a participatory qualitative approach. But, even then, one problem remains: the quality of care between households and communities differs a great deal—an aspect that can never be captured adequately by quantitative methods. Notwithstanding these limitations, getting a sense of household's capacity through some objective and easily computable[21] indicators may be a useful starting point for assessing a household's ability to absorb orphans in a specific context or location. Such an approach also may prove useful in helping target priority zones for support interventions.

Table 3.4 sums up the strengths and weaknesses of the various caregivers reviewed in this chapter. The table reveals that not one single arrangement can be touted with confidence as "the best arrangement." Yet the table gives some sense of what to expect from each caregiving arrangement, so that policymakers are aware of the potential problems in each arrangement and are able to supplement them with the appropriate interventions—an aspect to which we turn in the next chapter.

Although ranking remains difficult, because each type of arrangement has its pros and cons, there is a common acknowledgment that, whenever possible, orphaned siblings should remain together and with their kin and in their community of origin. When relatives are not available, placement in families willing to adopt or foster a child is the most appropriate solution. Institutions should always be considered a last resort, and small-scale foster homes should be favored over residential placements such as orphanages (figure 3.1). This way of perceiving desirable living arrangements is in line with the UN Convention of the Rights of the Child.

Figure 3.1. Ranking of Living Arrangements for Orphans

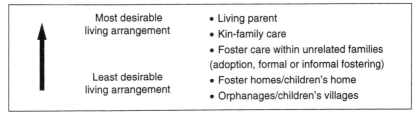

	Most desirable living arrangement	• Living parent
		• Kin-family care
		• Foster care within unrelated families (adoption, formal or informal fostering)
	Least desirable living arrangement	• Foster homes/children's home
		• Orphanages/children's villages

Table 3.4 Propensity of Caregivers to Meet Orphans' Needs

Needs \ Caregivers	Living parents	Grand-parents	Other relatives	Child household head	Foster family Formal	Foster family Informal	Adoption	Foster Home	Children's village	Orphanage
Basic needs										
– Shelter	High	High	High	Low	High	High	High	High	High	High
– Food	Low	Low	Low	Low	High	Low	High	High	High	High
– Access to health care	Low	Low	Low	Low	High	Low	High	High	High	High
– Clothing	Low	Low	Low	Low	High	Low	High	High	High	High
– Education	Low	Low	Low	Low	High	Low	High	High	High	High
Economic needs										
– Productive skills (training, vocational education)	Low	Low	Low	Low	High	Low	High	High	High	Low
– Income-generating activities	n.a.	n.a.	n.a.	Low	n.a.	n.a.	n.a.	n.a.	n.a.	n.a.
– Farm/productive inputs	n.a.	n.a.	n.a.	Low	n.a	n.a.	n.a.	n.a.	n.a.	n.a.
Safety needs										
– Protection from										
– verbal abuse	High	High	Risk	Low	High	Risk	High	High	Risk	Risk
– physical abuse	High	High	Risk	Low	High	Risk	High	High	Risk	Risk
– sexual abuse	High	High	Risk	Low	High	Risk	High	High	Risk	Risk
– work exploitation	Low	Low	Low	Low	High	Low	High	High	High	High

(Continued)

Legal needs									
– Property inheritance right	Low	Low	Low	Low	Low	Low	High	n.a.	n.a.	n.a.
Psychological and emotional needs										
– Loving environment (sense of attachment)	High	High	High	High	High	High	High	Risk	Risk	Low
– Caring environment	Low	High	Low	Low	High	Risk	High	High	High	Low
– Psychological and emotional support	Low	Low	High	Low	High	High	High	High	Risk	Low
– Socialization	High	High	High	Risk	High	High	High	High	Risk	Low

Source: The authors.

n.a. = Not applicable.

Note: "High" indicates the need is fulfilled; "low" indicates the need is not fulfilled; "risk" indicates there is a risk that the need will not be fulfilled.

Notes

1. This classification omits orphans who are living neither in a household nor in an institution, such as street children. These children, still a minority, are difficult to disentangle both empirically and operationally from other street children.

2. Child fostering is a practice in which children are reared by people other than their biological parents. Child fostering within family lines is sometimes called informal fostering (as opposed to formal fostering), whereby arrangements are made within the family without the involvement of any legal entities.

3. Indeed, "crisis fosterage is more a normative social obligation, rather than the politically and economically motivated rationale" (Aspaas 1999).

4. As discussed later, some interventions conducted mainly by nongovernmental organizations and community-based organizations have provided affected families with home-based care, economic support, memory books, psychological counseling, and legal protection for property and inheritance.

5. Uncles and aunts do sometimes refuse to foster their relatives' orphans because of the potential reduction in their own children's welfare. To avoid any complaint of neglect, they may prefer to leave this responsibility to other family members.

6. In some southern African countries (e.g., Botswana, Namibia, South Africa, Zimbabwe), a noncontributory social pension is in place. However, such pensions vary greatly in coverage, support, and effectiveness.

7. Indeed, the Uganda survey was conducted in a particularly vulnerable zone, hard-hit by HIV/AIDS and war. The first cases of child-headed households in communities affected by AIDS were reported in the late 1980s in Uganda and Tanzania (Foster and others 1997a). In Rwanda, child-headed households are estimated at 45,000 (World Vision 1998, cited by Subbarao, Mattimore, and Plangemann 2001).

8. Outside support is fairly limited for double orphans in rural Tanzania—9.5 percent (Urassa and others 1997)—but it seems more available (37 percent) for child- or adolescent-headed households in the Manicaland region of Zimbabwe (Foster and others 1997a). The ability of kin to provide the child-headed household with visits and material support depends on their location (must not live too far) and their own resources, respectively.

9. Frederick Luzze, from http://www.allafrica.com/stories/printable/20021108541. html (November 2002).

10. Fostering generally refers to a temporary arrangement, whereas adoption is generally viewed as a permanent one (Uppard and Petty 1998). In Malawi, out of the 44,000 orphans identified and receiving some kind of assistance in 1998, 43 were formally fostered by alien families and 4 were adopted (Kalemba 1998). In Zimbabwe, some 755 formal foster parents were caring for just over 1,000 children. The number of adoptions in one year was 45 (Parry 1998). It is assumed that the number of orphans formally fostered and then adopted has increased. However, its magnitude still remains low.

11. Faith-based organizations as well as nongovernmental organizations may also be part of the placement and supervision processes.

12. Indeed, such a legal vacuum may be an open door to unsanctioned child abuse. Yet even when laws and policies protecting children are enacted, they are often poorly enforced and therefore ineffective. Several reasons may account for this situation: (a) judiciary institutions and complaint mechanisms are inadequate or inaccessible (underbudgeted, under- and poorly staffed, urban-based); (b) children's rights are not known or are not well understood by the public; and (c) legal laws and policies may not be compatible with traditional laws and customs (Barrett 1998).

13. In South Africa, prospective parents follow a selective process in which their resources, stability, age, and marital bond are examined. Their ability to provide for the child and not depend on external resources is essential. This procedure has led adoption agencies to tend to favor middle-class adopters at the expense of poorer families (Brink 1998). In Kenya, the prospective parent or parents must be of good reputation, in a position to take care of a child, present a satisfactory home and living conditions—indeed, a home that is likely to meet the particular needs of the foster child (Adhiambo Ogwang 2001).

14. The ratio of social workers to the population is often 1:100,000 or even less (Hunter 2000).

15. In South Africa, the need for secrecy expressed by black South African families who want to adopt may not fit into the current transparent practice of adoption (Brink 1998). Indeed, most adoption and fostering policies and laws in South Africa, like those all over Sub-Saharan Africa, stem from former colonies' legal codes, which are not necessarily compatible with traditional customs and practices. In addition, the inadequacy or unavailability of adoption and fostering services hamper adoption, and, as noted, welfare bureaus are often poorly equipped and under- and poorly staffed.

16. More specifically, the child is part of the foster family and is taken care of and protected, but is not considered to be an official family member (Parry 1998).

17. The Rwandan government extends "orphan grants" to promote fostering by unrelated families. Yet very few households effectively receive this support: the percentage of double orphans is estimated at 13 percent of children under 15, but only 2 percent of households fostering orphans have received a grant (Siaens, Subbarao, and Wodon 2003).

18. Within this framework, some countries are trying to reintegrate children from institutions into society through reunification and rehabilitation programs for older orphans.

19. To render children's growth process as normal as possible (by avoiding isolation and stigmatization), it is best to establish close links between the children's village and the neighborhood community. An even better solution is to let children evolve in their own community by promoting instead children's homes.

20. When the neighborhood community shares a part of the cost of a children's village, it promotes ownership, reduces dependency on donors, and renders the intervention sustainable over time.

21. A simplified version of the indicator, by relying on a subset of indicators developed in table 3.3, can be developed to make its use easier in the field and to better reflect local needs and constraints.

CHAPTER 4

Interventions and Public Action to Strengthen Community Action

A s described in earlier chapters, the community-level coping mechanisms for orphan care vary a great deal, depending on the local situation. In general, communities make every effort to preserve the traditional safety net of the extended family, especially in rural areas. However, the magnitude of the orphan crisis, the spread of nuclear families in urban areas, and the additional hardships imposed by periodic droughts or floods (e.g., in Ethiopia, Malawi, and Mozambique) are probably weakening the traditional safety net in some countries and regions. Evidence also indicates that the practice of uncles and aunts (close relatives) taking on orphan care has lessened in some countries. Children who slip through the traditional safety net end up as street children or working children or live in child-headed households (Foster and Williamson 2000).

When the traditional safety net begins to weaken, the appropriate policy response depends on the country situation. Surely attempts must be made, through suitable public interventions, to strengthen and preserve the extended family as the first line of defense. Where the extended family has been stretched beyond its capacity—and field experience suggests that in some countries orphans are being "passed on" from one relative to another, thereby endangering the orphans' welfare— alternative arrangements are often sought, but these arrangements need not take the form of Western-style ones (e.g., orphanages, legal adoption). Some countries are already trying other arrangements that are more in line with the African cultural context, such as children's group homes in Eritrea and elsewhere (see chapter 3).

Even though the case for some sort of intervention is overwhelming, no standard package of established knowledge describing how to intervene in behalf of orphans and vulnerable children (OVC), what kind of assistance makes sense, and how to channel this assistance is available. Some studies do, however, provide very insightful generic guidelines on how to intervene in behalf of OVC. The "12 Principles for Programming" endorsed by the UNAIDS (Joint United Nations Programme on HIV/AIDS) Committee of Co-sponsoring Organizations, as well as the UNGASS (United Nations General Assembly Special Session) Declaration of Commitment on HIV/AIDS, especially Articles 65–67, which deal with children's support, offer a consensus framework for directing interventions aimed at support- ing OVC. Appendix E summarizes those principles and articles. The Millennium Development Goals also provide benchmarks that help those crafting interventions. In addition, several studies and reports written by implementing agencies—especially international nongovernmental organi- zations (NGOs) such as Alliance, Save the Children, World Vision, Plan International—and field workers offer valuable practical guidelines and tools on how to assist OVC at the grassroots level as well as at the regional, national, and global levels.[1] Finally, the plentiful information available on a variety of interventions related to circumstances in different countries can be used to suggest what kinds of interventions and channels might work in a given situation in a country.

In this chapter, we will review the types of interventions that are more suitable for addressing the needs of OVC living within family-like set- tings and among communities. In particular, we will review the different options available to strengthen the caregiving capacity of the different actors currently looking after orphans—options that can be supported with public or donor funds. Then we will turn to a discussion of the pros and cons of alternative institutional responses, with particular reference to the issue of sustainability.

Addressing the Needs of OVC Living in Family-Like Settings

No matter the nature and intensity of publicly provided support, the family remains the predominant caring unit for orphans and vulnerable children in much of Africa.[2] Although the vast majority of Africans remain HIV-negative, a growing number of families are bound to be overwhelmed by the strain caused by HIV/AIDS deaths as the HIV/AIDS toll increases. Spontaneous responses have burgeoned within communities as they seek to prevent orphans and households from falling into destitution. Some community initiatives have taken a more formal form, eventually becoming community-based organizations (CBOs). Today, faith-based organizations (FBOs), local NGOs, CBOs, and community groups, such as women's-groups, youth clubs, and people living with HIV and AIDS (PLWHA) groups, are at the front line of support for OVC. Most of these vulnerable children are supported by national and international NGOs, governments, and donors.[3]

Preventing Children from Becoming Orphans

Preventing children from becoming orphans should be the first critically important strategy adopted by governments, NGOs, and donors. Different ways have proven effective in preventing the number of orphans from rising. They include: preventing unwanted pregnancies, reducing maternal mortality, preventing HIV transmission, and enabling PLWHA to live longer (Hunter 2000). Family planning services, voluntary counseling and testing (VCT) facilities, antiretroviral (ARV) therapy, and health care services for women are major interventions that could greatly help to reduce the incidence of orphanhood (table 4.1) by, among other things,[4] prolonging the life of HIV-positive parents. The World Bank's multicountry AIDS programs (MAPs) have a major role to play in improving access to these interventions by helping to fund projects such as prevention activities and ARV therapy for PLWHA.

Improving the Financial Situation of Caregivers

The reluctance of some extended families to take on the responsibility of orphans stems in part from the inadequate financial resources of the extended family. Helping affected families to strengthen their income base is often viewed as a prerequisite to placing orphans in a secure

Table 4.1 Ways to "Prevent" Orphans

Way to prevent orphans	Intervention
Reduce births	– Continue/intensify family planning education. – Encourage directed counseling for HIV-positive women considering pregnancy. – Make family planning methods widely available, including barrier methods and condoms to prevent HIV transmission. – Provide youths with schooling and economic opportunities.*
Reduce maternal mortality	– Make family planning more available to reduce fertility and associated ob/gyn problems. – Improve women's access to health care services. – Legalize abortions, reducing nonmedical interventions.
Prevent HIV transmission	– Make infection rates widely known. – Make (voluntary*) counseling and testing widely available. – Provide widespread sexually transmitted disease (STD) diagnosis and treatment. – Encourage change in sexual behavior. – Provide schooling and economic opportunities for youths, especially young women.* – Provide training in life skills for youth and promote peer education.
Support PLWHA so they can live longer	– Reduce discrimination and stigma. – Ensure access to medical care (especially ARV therapy). – Encourage good nutrition. – Reduce stress, including concern about surviving children.

Sources: Hunter (2000) and authors (*).

setting that can be sustained over the medium term. A variety of mechanisms can be used to stabilize or increase households' income. The most popular responses developed by the different actors are labor sharing, home and communal gardening, a switch to less risky–less productive types of activities, diversification of the source of revenue (e.g., diversifying crops, productive activities), microfinance, income-generating activities, provision of marketable skills through training of out-of-school children, and cash or in-kind transfers (tables 4.2 and 4.3).

But how sustainable are these measures aimed at augmenting the resources available to extended families looking after orphans? Table 4.3 presents the advantages and disadvantages associated with each intervention. Microfinance and income-generating activities (IGAs) are often viewed as important means of strengthening households' economic

Table 4.2 Responses Developed by Stakeholders to Meet Needs of OVC Living in Family-Like Settings

Need to be met	Community/household	Nongovernmental organizations	Government
		Level of intervention	
Prevent children from becoming orphans	– Encourage the use of family planning methods. – Encourage counseling for HIV-positive women. – Promote voluntary testing. – Promote safe sexual behavior. – Provide young people with life skills, peer education.	– Provide family planning education and methods. – Provide and improve access to VCT services. – Distribute ARV therapy to PLWHA. – Provide youths (especially women) with training, access to income, and economic opportunities. – Provide young people with life skills, peer education.	– Provide family planning education and methods (especially condoms). – Improve women's access to health care services. – Improve access to VCT services. – Improve access of PLWHA to ARV therapy. – Provide youths, especially young women, with schooling, access to income, and economic opportunities.
Improve household income	– Promote labor sharing. – Undertake home gardening and communal gardens (when appropriate). – Resort to less labor-intensive and more stress-resistant crops. – Resort to less risky, less productive activities. – Establish savings clubs (ROSCAs). – Undertake income-generating activities. – Seek marketable skills training for out-of-school youth. – Promote multiple farming systems and multicropping.	– Initiate cash/in-kind transfer to affected families. – Undertake microfinance (formal savings and credit schemes, in-kind revolving credit). – Promote income-generating activities. – Help with product marketing. – Provide agricultural assistance—in-kind (seeds, tools) and technical. – Promote agricultural training and support for young people and widows. – Promote agricultural techniques that use locally available inputs and are adapted to farmers' existing resource base.	– Initiate cash/in-kind transfers to affected families (grants to foster families). – Provide agricultural assistance to communities (in-kind and technical). – Promote agricultural techniques that use locally available inputs and are adapted to farmers' existing resource base. – Promote agricultural training and support for young people and widows. – Help to establish multiple farming systems and multicropping. – Provide marketable skills training for out-of-school youths.

(Continued)

Table 4.2 Responses Developed by Stakeholders to Meet Needs of OVC Living in Family-Like Settings (*Continued*)

Need to be met	Level of intervention		
	Community/household	Nongovernmental organizations	Government
		– Help to establish multiple farming systems and multicropping. – Provide marketable skills training for out-of-school children.	
Adequate basic needs			
General		– Ensure home visits to monitor the well-being of the child. – Raise awareness of OVC's needs.	
Shelter	– Initiate community house repairs.	– Provide inputs.	– Give grants to the neediest households.
Food	– Improve access to and the availability of food (home gardens, improved agricultural production and its marketing, communal gardens). – Enhance effective nutrition practices, supplementary food programs, nutrition counseling (especially for child-headed households). – Give food rations to the neediest children. – Promote school feeding programs and school gardens.	– Provide technical assistance (seed selection, irrigation, natural resources management). – Provide agricultural inputs. – Train nutrition counselors. – Provide food for feeding programs.	– Offer technical assistance for better farming practices. – Support public health workers who will provide training in nutrition. – Give food baskets to foster families.
Health care	– Distribute medicines to the neediest households. – Establish rural pharmacies. – Open day care centers, youth clubs (to address adolescents' specific needs, HIV/AIDS prevention). – Provide home-based care for PLWHA. – Provide hospital referral.	– Distribute medicines to the neediest households. – Provide inputs for rural pharmacies. – Train health counselors. – Provide material for basic hygiene (soap). – Support home-based care for PLWHA. – Support hospital referral.	– Provide health subsidies for OVC. – Support public health workers who will provide training in health issues. – Launch immunization campaigns for all children.

Clothing	– Collect used clothing to hand over to needy children.		– Provide grants for OVC.
Education	– Engage in economic strengthening to enable households to pay school fees. – Support community fund-raising to send OVC children to school. – Bear school-related expenses. – Provide in-kind support for schools that admit OVC. – Collect used uniforms, shoes, and books for OVC in need. – Enable OVC to attend school without uniforms. – Promote alternative forms of education: distant learning, community schools, interactive radio education. – Provide training in marketable skills for out-of-school youths (especially for child-headed households). – Support preschool programs for children 3–6 years old.	– Support school subsidies (fees, books, uniforms). – Ensure that cash granted to the neediest guardian is tied to child's attendance at school (conditional cash transfers). – Promote alternative forms of education: distant learning, community schools, interactive radio education. – Support vocational training and informal education for youth. – Provide agricultural training and support for young people. – Support preschool programs for children 3–6 years old.	– Provide school subsidies for fees, books, and uniforms. – Waive fees and uniforms for OVC. – Eliminate school fees and uniforms for all children. – Ensure that cash granted to guardian is tied to child's attendance at school (conditional cash transfers). – Promote alternative forms of education: distant learning, community schools, interactive radio education. – Improve quality of education. – Support vocational training and informal education for youth. – Provide agricultural training and support for young people. – Support preschool programs for children 3–6 years old.

Safety needs

General		– Raise awareness of OVC's safety needs.	
Prevention of verbal/physical/ sexual abuse	– Arrange home visits to monitor OVC's well-being. – Ensure referrals to the appropriate social services.	– Train volunteers and local professional (e.g., teachers, nurses, religious bodies) to recognize abuse of children and refer abused children to the appropriate social services. – Ensure referrals to the appropriate social services.	– Enact a law against child abuse and enforce it. – Enforce reprisals against child abuse. – Strengthen social services.

(Continued)

Table 4.2 Responses Developed by Stakeholders to Meet Needs of OVC Living in Family-Like Settings (Continued)

Need to be met	Level of intervention		
	Community/household	Nongovernmental organizations	Government
Prevention of work exploitation	– Arrange home visits to monitor OVC's well-being. – Arrange home helpers to reduce workloads of vulnerable children.	– Train volunteers to recognize child abuse and address the issue.	– Implement and enforce the appropriate laws. – Enforce reprisals against households that exploit OVC.
Legal needs			
General	– Promote advocacy and raise awareness about property and inheritance rights.		
Property inheritance rights	– Facilitate written wills and birth and death registration. – Promote allocation of land by traditional leaders to landless households (those who experienced property grabbing or do not have access to their land because of displacement or insecurity).	– Support OVC and widows. – Facilitate wills. – Facilitate transition/guardianship.	– Establish legal support to enforce children's rights. – Enforce reprisals against offenders. – Establish the practice of written wills and birth and death registration.
Psychological and emotional needs	– Incorporate counseling through home visits by volunteers to orphans and their caretakers (and especially for children living with dying parents). – Favor recreational activities such as storytelling by the elderly, sports, and the arts (e.g., dance, painting, drawing, songs). – Promote youth clubs. – Develop community services and communal eating (where adults and children are together). – Prepare the family for planning for the future of the child when parents are dying.	– Train community volunteers to provide orphans and their caretakers with emotional and psychological support. – Train local professionals (e.g., teachers, nurses, religious bodies, traditional healers) to recognize the needs of OVC and provide care.	– Include psychological support in teacher training programs. – Support home visits by trained public health personnel.

Source: The authors.

Note: ARV = antiretroviral; VCT = voluntary counseling and testing; ROSCA = rotating savings and credit association; PLWHA = people living with HIV/AIDS.

Table 4.3 Interventions to Improve the Financial Situation of Families Fostering Orphans and Vulnerable Children

Intervention	Advantage	Drawback
Labor sharing	– Frees caregivers and children for performing other tasks. – Enhances community cohesion (especially valuable in postconflict settings). – Community possesses ownership of the initiative.	– May not be sustainable in high-prevalence areas because HIV/AIDS epidemic depletes human resources. – May overburden some community members.
Communal gardening	– Restores an ancient tradition. – Enhances community cohesion. – Is a source of resources for landless households (important for displaced/refugee households). – Ownership of the initiative rests with the community.	– May overburden some community members (especially because the HIV/AIDS epidemic depletes human resources).
Home gardening	– Improves income as well as food security. – Improves individual skills.	– May overburden women and increase child labor.
Development of less labor-intensive and more stress-resistant crops (such as cassava)	– Improves income as well as food security. – Improves individual skills.	– Fosters dependency on external assistance for providing seed and technical assistance. Yet this risk is minimized when cuttings are provided (i.e., communities can develop crop nurseries).
Agricultural assistance (use of new crops, natural pesticides, irrigation)	– Improves community members' skills.	– Fosters dependency on external assistance.
Microfinance	– Improves access to credit and savings schemes. – Reduces vulnerability to loss. – Enables avoidance of irreversible coping strategies. – Enables initiation of income-generating activities.	– Skills are needed to manage money (may lead to unsustainable level of indebtedness). – Does not reach the neediest households (not appropriate for destitute households). – Requires follow-up.

(Continued)

Table 4.3 Interventions to Improve the Financial Situation of Families Fostering Orphans and Vulnerable Children (*Continued*)

Intervention	Advantage	Drawback
In-kind revolving credit (cattle, poultry)	– Is easy to implement. – Enhances food security.	– May create more vulnerability if the animal dies, because it is an "indivisible good."
Income-generating activities	– Diversifies sources of income.	– Requires adequate skills and market opportunities. – Relies on external assistance to help find markets and to get adequate training. – Has low rate of success.
Marketable skills training (including apprenticeship) for out-of-school youths	– Improves skills and is particularly adequate for adolescent household heads and youths living with sick or old caregivers.	– Relies on external trainers. Yet this risk may be mitigated if one relies on local apprenticeship training.
Cash/in-kind transfers to needy households	– May be particularly adequate for destitute households (child-headed households, OVC living with sick parents or old caregivers).	– May be difficult to manage if the number of potential beneficiaries increases substantially. – Households may become dependent on such aid relief. – May not directly improve the OVC well-being. – May not be financially sustainable over the long run (especially as the HIV/AIDS epidemic increases the number of needy households). – Government has limited resources to provide for all the destitute.

Sources: The authors and Plan International and others (2001).

resources on a sustainable basis, independent from external assistance. The performance of microfinance and IGA activities varies widely, and robust evidence on whether these schemes provide significant positive impacts on orphans is lacking, although recent evaluations do point to some positive household-level impacts. In general, microfinance and IGA activities might be much less successful in unfavorable environments characterized by pervasive poverty, sharply depleted human and economic resources (in high HIV/AIDS-prevalent regions), and political instability and insecurity (in postconflict countries).[5]

Information about the impacts of microfinance institutions (MFIs) in the HIV/AIDS context is thin and patchy at best. Indeed, it is difficult to draw any firm conclusions about microfinance because it is, in turn, difficult to assess the HIV status of clients and disentangle the impact of HIV/AIDS itself from its economic impacts on affected clients' activities. An explanatory study from Zambuko MFI in Zimbabwe provides, however, some insightful information (Barnes 2002). The analysis shows clearly that microfinance helps clients' households better manage the negative economic effects of AIDS. Compared with nonclients affected by the disease, affected clients enjoyed a greater number of income sources, enabling them to better smooth their consumption. The study also reveals that a higher proportion of boys ages 6–16 living in HIV-affected client households were attending school (Barnes 2002). Improved access to education—and to a lesser extent to health care—is emerging as the most valued result of access to microfinance services. Evidence from the Ugandan Women's Effort to Save Orphans (UWESO) shows that when microfinance is carried out appropriately, foster families may greatly benefit from its services. An impact evaluation of the UWESO Savings and Credit Schemes (USCS) revealed that foster families have improved their daily meal intakes, upgraded their housing, and increased their material welfare. USCS also has enabled more orphans to go to school, whether at primary level or secondary level (White 2002).

Although "financial services may reduce the vulnerability of poor individuals and households by providing access to 'chunks' of money to protect against risk and cope with shocks" (Wright and others 1999),[6] it is doubtful that microfinance can be regarded as a panacea for the orphan problem, nor can it be assumed that it is suitable for all types of households in all locations. Two related questions are pertinent: Do the benefits of successful microfinance activities in fostering households actually percolate down to orphans? And if so, do microfinance initiatives succeed in poverty-stricken, high-prevalence HIV areas? Assuming the answer to the first question is positive, microfinance institutions are faced with new challenges as the HIV epidemic continues to spread (Parker 2000):

- The increased difficulty that HIV/AIDS-affected or -infected clients will encounter in trying to repay their loans while having to devote more time to taking care of ill household members or becoming themselves too ill to work

- Changes in the MFI's portfolio quality after rising loan delinquency, particularly if affected households have been encouraged to borrow beyond their ability to repay

- The increased costs of maintaining or expanding the MFI's client base as the number of exiting clients rises

- Increased MFI costs as staff members themselves are affected or infected by the virus (causing higher staff turnover and absenteeism).

Appropriate measures such as the provision of short-term loans, transferable loans, emergency funds, or insurance schemes can help to sustain microfinance activities in heavily affected HIV zones.

MFI can contribute effectively in many ways (reviewed in appendix F) toward mitigating the adverse impacts of HIV/AIDS by supporting both households with HIV patients and fostering households. How and whether these initiatives actually benefit orphans will be revealed only through carefully structured evaluations. Clearly, then, more needs to be learned.

Improving foster families' material situation will without a doubt enhance their capacity to cope adequately with orphans and vulnerable children. Microfinance is just one important option, provided that one is confident that the poorest households will really become successful entrepreneurs if assistance is channeled. Because the likelihood of the very poorest benefiting from microfinance is not high,[7] more specific interventions may be necessary to ensure the welfare of orphans and vulnerable children in very poor households.

Addressing OVC's Basic Needs

Here again a range of responses have flourished within communities aimed at helping affected families to address the basic needs of orphans and vulnerable children (table 4.2). Four general observations are in order about these responses. First, because of lack of monitoring and evaluation systems, as yet no studied success stories have emerged on the sustainability (financial and otherwise) and impact of these initiatives. Second, most of these initiatives have been sporadic and piecemeal, rather than well-conceived, well-funded nationwide programs. Third, these initiatives are more developmental (e.g., income-generating activities for households) than specific to the needs of orphans. And, fourth, where cash is involved, the potential for abuse (misappropriation) cannot be ruled out. One important point neglected in the literature is that these initiatives place an undue burden on caregivers, *especially women*. General developmental schemes—that is, those that improve access to basic services, such as a piped water supply, fuel-efficient stoves (which reduce the time required to collect firewood), and day care centers fully staffed and funded—can reduce caregivers' burdens and benefit the whole community as much as specific initiatives aimed at targeted extended families. It is very important to be vigilant that these specific initiatives do not crowd out the general developmental schemes, especially the resources going to health and education. Close monitoring of orphan-specific initiatives is needed to ensure that they do not place an excessive burden on caregivers in general and women in particular.

Of particular importance are two broad categories of interventions: (a) school subsidies, vouchers, and fee waivers; and (b) health and nutrition interventions aimed at OVC. Interventions aimed at ensuring that orphans enjoy the same probability of enrollment in school as children with living parents fall into two large categories. The first is broadly sector-specific interventions that benefit *all* children, including orphans. Examples are abolishing school fees, improving school quality, revising a curriculum, and offering school feeding programs. The second category is orphan-specific interventions such as school-related subsidies or school vouchers, or in-kind support to schools admitting disproportionate numbers of orphans and vulnerable children.[8] Clearly, abolition of school fees and school uniforms benefits all children, and especially orphans living in resource-constrained households or environments. Evidence suggests that policies such as universal primary education (UPE) did remove potential disadvantages faced by orphans in Uganda (Deininger, Garcia, and Subbarao 2003).[9] But evidence on the effectiveness of other general programs, such as school feeding or nutrition and school enrollments, is rather thin.

Less well known are the impacts of orphan-specific interventions. Most interventions that directly favor orphans' access to education are recent ones that have not been evaluated for their effectiveness.[10] Decentralization of the implementation of programs aimed directly at orphans may have a high degree of success if communities are actively involved, although external checks and balances may still be required.

As for health and nutrition interventions, preschool children in households with adults suffering from AIDS morbidity will require food supplementation either in the form of distribution on a temporal basis from agencies such as the World Food Program, or through investments in gardening (distribution of seeds and tools), or through distribution of small livestock (such as chickens and goats) or even cattle (this was an experiment in the Eritrea Early Childhood Project). Nutrition education also can play a significant role. It is important as well to ensure that such children receive immunization shots like all other children. Evidence suggests that because of stigma or bias on the part of health workers, or for other reasons, when compared with other children, a much lower percentage of children whose parents have AIDS received immunizations (Deininger, Garcia, and Subbarao 2003). Although civil society and community organizations can and do intervene in the short run to remove this bias against orphans, in the medium term program delivery of basic health, nutrition, and education services to vulnerable children should form part of the public policy, duly funded in national budgets. Decentralized investments specially targeted to orphans and vulnerable children can be implemented through earmarked grants to local authorities, who, in consultation with communities, will have to ensure the targeting and cost-effectiveness of the grants. It is hard to conceptualize any other medium-term option.

As for other initiatives in support of orphans (such as for shelter or clothing), they should be undertaken with caution, trying to avoid stigmatizing the children. In general, sector-specific policies aimed at meeting basic needs and benefiting all orphans and vulnerable children—and implemented in a decentralized fashion with community grants—seem to be the preferred option compared with orphan-specific interventions.

That said, three needs that require truly orphan-specific interventions are worth mentioning: (a) ensuring safety and preventing abuse; (b) meeting legal needs; and (c) providing psychosocial support.

Addressing OVC's Safety Needs

Home visits by community volunteers are the backbone of efforts to monitor the well-being of OVC. When adequately run, community-based orphan care may produce very positive impacts for orphans and their caretakers. Evidence from FOCUS in Zimbabwe shows that children gain emotional, spiritual, and material support from the FOCUS volunteers.[11] Because the volunteers are often viewed as a mother or a grandmother, they help to improve the integration of the children into community life and are able to better address difficult issues such as sexual abuse (Lee 2000).

Currently, however, in most countries home visits present many flaws:

• Visits are often fragmented and made on an ad hoc basis

• Visits are carried out by concerned persons from NGOs and CBOs but by very few persons from the public sector

• Home visit programs are hampered by stigma, denial, fear, and secrecy

• Volunteers lack the skills required to recognize and address abuse and psychological issues in an effective way[12]

• The number of volunteers is insufficient

• It is difficult to sustain volunteer motivation when the workload increases substantially

• Functional referral systems are unavailable in cases of abuse.[13]

Although legislation against abuse is in place in most countries, implementation is lax, and governments appear to see no need for any additional steps other than for enforcement of the laws, including reprisal actions when necessary. Yet the welfare of children in general and orphans in particular is not guaranteed if (a) judiciary institutions and complaint mechanisms are inadequate or inaccessible (that is, underbudgeted, under- and badly staffed, urban-based); (b) children's rights are not known or are not well understood by the public; and (c) the legal framework is not compatible with traditional laws and customs. In such a context, leaders of civil societies, religious leaders, and faith-based organizations have an important role to play in advocating and raising awareness on this issue and in ensuring that the child protection laws are revised as needed and then enforced. In Burundi, community leaders and the traditional authority—*Bashingantahe* and *Nyumbakumi*—have been asked to identify cases of abuse and devise the appropriate solutions. It is only in unresolved cases that judiciary authorities are to intervene.

External support is also required to provide home visitors with adequate training and material support. Yet no blueprint exists on the content of such training and how it should be conducted. Practices vary widely according to who is implementing them (NGOs, FBOs, CBOs, or others) and with what resources. Nevertheless, as underlined by Williamson and Donahue (2001) in their assessment of the COPE project in Malawi, "providing quality care requires hands-on training by qualified people, not class-room lectures." Guidelines and standards on issues such as how to effectively recognize and address abuse issues by volunteer visitors, how to manage and coordinate the work of volunteers, and how to conduct such training should be designed by qualified local actors with the technical assistance of NGOs and widely disseminated. In addition, other issues should systematically be given more emphasis. They include: (a) addressing the stigmatization of and discrimination against orphans; (b) increasing children's participation in the projects that target them; (c) making volunteers more attentive to orphans' needs and desires; and (d) encouraging successful NGOs to shift from an implementing role to a facilitating one in building the capacity of CBOs and local NGOs.[14]

The issue of sustaining the motivation of volunteers over the long run also deserves special attention. As volunteers are asked to take on more and more work, they may reach a saturation point, which could threaten to break down the whole system. Therefore, some authors and practitioners have advocated providing trained volunteers with a certificate (enhancing their self-esteem) and remuneration. Such a step would be an opportunity to create "expanded employment in basic services for new cadres of community-based paraprofessionals who can provide outreach services and support to children, families and communities" (Hunter 2000). Yet some country-specific experiences show that members of local associations, religious communities, or local traditional authorities can be pursued to work without pay, or with very little material incentive. FOCUS (Lee 2000) and COPE in Malawi (Mann 2002) are insightful examples of that process.[15]

Addressing OVC's Legal Needs

Raising communities' recognition that widows and orphans need security of tenure is a first step toward the legal needs of OVC. In some countries such as Swaziland, communities have begun to advocate children's inheritance rights, and traditional authorities have begun allocating lands to this vulnerable group (FM&G 2002). In Mozambique, Namibia, and Tanzania, land tenure systems and property ownership have been opened up to women (Hunter 2000). The responsibility here rests squarely on governments; they must establish birth and death certificates and enforce inheritance rights for orphans, among other things. These efforts of governments should be complemented by civil society initiatives to ensure succession planning and to encourage families to write their wills to counter property grabbing. In Uganda, memory books written by dying parents have proven to effectively support both wills and succession planning. Again, community volunteers and local leaders must play a major role in this matter.[16]

Addressing OVC's Psychological and Emotional Needs

A wide range of interventions—though patchy and most often limited in outreach—are available for (foster) parents, vulnerable children, and orphans. Counseling is provided by volunteer home visitors, day care centers, youth clubs, schools, and religious groups. Yet psychological assistance is by far the most difficult service to provide, mainly because few trained men and women are in the villages and because the need is largely intangible and thus often underestimated or ignored. One option is to train community volunteers, teachers,[17] nurses, and traditional healers to monitor, assign priority to, and address the psychological and emotional needs of both parents and OVC. Foster parents are often unaware of orphans' emotional and psychological needs, and they find themselves puzzled when facing orphans' sorrow and asocial behaviors. It is critical that they better understand the mourning process, the importance of nurturing and safe attachment, and the need to keep siblings together. In particular, children living with dying parents[18] need close supervision and counseling. Indeed, one study found that in Zambia the children of sick parents are significantly more likely to show signs of psychological disturbance than children without sick parents (Poulter 1997, cited by HUMULIZA / Terre des Hommes Switzerland 1999). A good option is to integrate OVC counseling support into programs for parents living with HIV/AIDS. In addition, integrating OVC care into home-based care, as noted earlier, has advantages: easier identification of abuse, supervision of school attendance, provision of counseling and advice on varied issues (e.g., sexual, stigmatization, discrimination), provision of basic health care, and referral to a community system when required.

Another important issue is promoting the social integration of orphans. They may face stigmas and discrimination, further exacerbating their feeling of loneliness and abandonment. To restore to them a sense of normalcy and security, activities that favor social interactions among children and between children and adults should be promoted and strengthened. Successful interventions include arranging recreational and spiritual activities such as play, storytelling by the elderly, sports, and art (dance, painting, drawing, singing); promoting youth clubs and peer group education; and developing community services and communal eating at which adults and children are together.

Again, there is no blueprint for what types of intervention are most effective. Because psychological needs are so broad and involve so many issues, organizations must devise the activities most appropriate to their setting. The review in box 4.1 of the psychological support offered to children affected by HIV/AIDS in Tanzania and Zimbabwe provides some examples of activities that are deemed relevant (UNAIDS 2001).

Box 4.1 Examples of Psychological Support Offered to Children Affected by HIV/AIDS in Tanzania and Zimbabwe

Educating Teachers: The HUMULIZA Pilot Project in Northwestern Tanzania
HUMULIZA provides counseling sessions and education seminars for primary school teachers and other NGOs on the importance of communicating with children. During these sessions, teachers are sensitized on (a) how to identify children's problems and needs, (b) the importance of attachment, and (c) how to improve a child's self-esteem. Positive results have emerged quickly: teachers have been able to identify the orphans' problems; the environment has become more conducive to children expressing their feelings; and class attendance has improved. In addition, teachers have extended their commitment by visiting orphans in their homes after class hours and following up on their progress. They also have discussed children's rights issues with the children's caregivers. Finally, teachers have created an orphan fund from their own salary, mainly to cover orphans' school supplies.

Learning Life Skills through Adventure: The Salvation Army's Masiye Camp
Participation in games and sports plays a major role in children's development and ability to release stress and better cope. The Masiye Camp in Zimbabwe provides vulnerable children (mainly child-headed households and children living with ill parents) with life skills through bush camps during school holidays. OVC are identified by other organizations, and counselors are volunteers (often orphans themselves). Activities range from hiking, canoeing, and abseiling to craft making, traditional dancing, and drama and fitness training.

Providing Ongoing Support for Children in Their Own Community: Youth for a Child in Christ (YOCIC)
YOCIC works with Masiye Camp to provide ongoing support to children in their communities. YOCIC is a youth initiative—managed and run by youth for youth—in support of children affected by AIDS and orphans in urban high-density communities. Started in 1998, YOCIC counted, as of 2001, 250 members who were supporting 1,650 orphans through various clubs that offer activities similar to those of the Masiye Camp—that is, the activities encourage children to build life skills and teamwork.

Source: UNAIDS (2001).

Although they do not deal directly with the issues surrounding orphans and vulnerable children affected by HIV/AIDS, studies of the psychological needs of children affected by armed conflict may provide very insightful approaches to how to address the HIV/AIDS issues in a practical manner. We reproduce here the basic principles and approaches suggested by the International Save the Children Alliance (1996)[19] for programs involving war-affected children, bearing in mind that similar interventions could be applied to orphans and vulnerable children affected by HIV/AIDS:

- Apply a long-term perspective that incorporates the psychological well-being of children

- Adopt a community-based approach that encourages self-help and builds on local culture, realities, and perceptions of child development

- Promote normal family and everyday life so as to reinforce a child's natural resilience

- Focus on primary care and prevention of further harm in the healing of children's psychological wounds

- Provide support as well as training for personnel who care for children

- Ensure clarity on ethical issues in order to protect children

- Advocate children's rights.

Addressing the Needs of OVC Living in Institutionalized Settings

Institutionalized care is one option for abandoned children and those who require special attention (e.g., HIV/AIDS-infected orphans, handicapped children, abused children). A screening device should be used to ensure that institutionalized care is resorted to only when no better placement options are available, and only as a temporary measure until a placement in a suitable family is arranged. The success of an orphanage resides not so much in keeping a child in it, but rather in the rapid placement of that child in a foster home.

Most institutions (orphanages, children's villages) tend to host a sizable number of children, usually about 200 or less. Two particular concerns about such institutions are whether the level of care provided meets the standards, and how to contain their excessive unit costs of care (see the next section for details). Evidence on the first concern is conflicting: the care provided by some institutions seems to be quite substantial and satisfactory, and especially by those institutions run by NGOs. For example, SOS Children's Village Lilongwe (Malawi) is part of an international movement of orphanages worldwide. Because SOS is a comparatively well-endowed NGO, the institution seems to be providing a comfortable environment for children—indeed, often too comfortable compared with local standards. But this is not true of all institutions and orphanages: abuse of children is not uncommon. As for their unit costs, as revealed in the next section, orphanages and children's villages are the most expensive form of care.

It is not surprising, then, that new, creative, and less institutional innovations are emerging in much of Africa, largely because of the dissatisfaction with the Western-style orphanages. These innovative approaches try to overcome the twin disadvantages (just noted) of the usual institutional care. One approach consists of small foster homes run by foster mothers in a children's community. The foster mothers are trained to better address the nutritional and psychological needs of OVC, and visits (by NGOs or community workers) to foster homes are encouraged to monitor children's welfare. The second approach is day-support programs for vulnerable children living with households.

But when institutional arrangements—especially orphanages and children's villages—become an imperative, what features should be sought for such institutional care? According to MacLeod (2001), these institutions should

- Be located in communities

- Replicate the local communities' levels of physical support and family structures, including the mingling of children in different age groups

- Promote children's contact with community and family members (by sending them to local schools and having them play with other children in the community) and involve children in the decisions affecting them

- Make available better trained staff in order to provide children with adequate care and psychological and emotional support

- Organize regular visits by civil society leaders so they can monitor these establishments

- Adhere to the national standards for institutional arrangements that should be established.

Rendering these residential care institutions as only a temporary place for OVC requires building up an effective tracking and reunification system for abandoned children who may still have living extended family members. In Zimbabwe, it appears that 75 percent of children living in institutions have a known relative (Powell 1999, cited by Phiri and Webb 2002). Yet tracking is very time-consuming and expensive, and inadequate information on parents and children, remote and inaccessible villages, and insecurity may lengthen the process. Moreover, some follow-up actions will be needed to ensure that a child receives adequate care once reunified with his or her family.

For abandoned children who have no suitable known guardians (that is, they have no known surviving kin, or they were abused in their foster families, or they are disabled), placements in family-type homes (preferably foster homes) should be favored over orphanages, because such homes offer a much better environment for children to develop.[20] An additional option is to place them in substitute families (e.g., fostering and adoption within alien families). But first a network of potential foster or adoptive families must be established and the capacity of social workers and social welfare systems strengthened. Promoting fosterage into unrelated families also would be necessary, but it would demand a shift in community members' beliefs and attitudes. When culturally feasible, traditional, religious, and political leaders should advocate such practices and raise awareness[21] of the need to foster abandoned children in societies where the number of OVC is increasing and that of extended family–based caregivers is shrinking. Many potential caregivers in different countries have expressed their willingness to foster alien children, and they have done so for material assistance. This situation raises fundamental questions about the appropriate choice of the caregiver and the types of incentives needed to channel assistance to OVC in a nonexploitative, nonstigmatizing manner.

Desirable Interventions to Support OVC and Their Families

Today in most Sub-Saharan African countries, the social impacts of the AIDS crisis, such as orphanhood and loss of breadwinners, are largely borne by families and communities with very few external resources. Public social welfare services, like communities, are overwhelmed because of poor and insufficient staff and resources, and so are unable to provide basic services to vulnerable children. Institutions, as described in this chapter, are playing a limited role, fostering at best 2–3 percent of orphans and often under unsatisfactory conditions.[22] In these circumstances, efforts must be directed toward strengthening the capacity of communities. Building community capacity also will have significant spillover benefits in countries where the decentralization process is being initiated.

Focusing First on Family and Community-Based Interventions

All interventions that encourage a situation in which children remain and grow up in their home environment should be given priority. Such measures could qualify as "preventive."[23] They are particularly cost-effective, enabling children to remain in their home and community. As costs are kept down, such interventions enable a larger number of orphans to be served by a limited budget, in sharp contrast to institutional placements for OVC.[24] However, providing sustained and adequate care and support to vulnerable children and orphans, especially in mature HIV/AIDS epidemic settings or war-torn countries, may become increasingly difficult, necessitating the evolution of innovative approaches to orphan care at the community level. Of particular concern is the issue of sustaining the motivation of volunteers over the long run. Although the involvement of volunteers remains the backbone of home-based services,[25] their workload has increased dramatically over time as the number of orphans has swelled. Risks of burnout among volunteers is a fear and should be thoroughly discussed with the volunteers and all those with whom they work. The best way to address the issue of sustainability of home-based care over time is to keep the costs under control and not undermine indigenous community coping mechanisms. Programs such as FOCUS have demonstrated that this is possible by relying on motivated, well-trained community volunteers and by providing limited material support to families such as seeds in the planting season and blankets in winter (Makufa 2001). Yet effective community mobilization and good community ownership remain critical. Involvement of political and traditional leaders, including religious leaders, as well as schools and the police, is part of this process. NGOs have a major role in facilitating such mobilization.

Other critical issues in most Sub-Saharan African countries are the lack of an appropriate and effective referral system for child abuse cases and the existence of strong but harmful traditional laws that sometimes conflict with formal laws, making it difficult to protect orphans' interests within exclusively volunteer-driven services. Although a volunteer system is a desirable way to provide assistance, significant monitoring is required not only to ensure appropriate care but also to protect legal rights, especially inheritance.

Relying on Direct In-Kind or Cash Transfers to Affected Groups When Necessary

Although sectoral policies seem to be the most appropriate tools for dealing with access to education and health and nutrition services, not all governments are (technically or financially) ready to provide all children with free access to schools and nutrition and basic health care services. Direct in-kind or cash transfers or fee waivers (vouchers) to affected groups may become necessary to ensure that these fundamental needs of the critically vulnerable children are met. As the number of OVC grow, it is important that only the *most vulnerable* children are targeted if transfers are to remain sustainable over the long term. Therefore, transfers must be managed at the local level through NGOs or CBOs, because they are more knowledgeable about local situations and needs and therefore are in a better position to identify the neediest OVC.

Transfers may also be relevant to attracting new parents and individuals into fostering and adoption practices. Indeed, it appears that in many countries families are willing to foster alien children if they receive some kind of support. The desired level of transfer—whether in kind or in cash—will have to be set in a way that prevents opportunistic behavior (such as that exhibited by poor families interested more in the benefits associated with fostering than in the care of the orphans) and upholds the sustainability of such an approach.

Table 4.4 Risks Faced by OVC and Interventions to Help Families Meet OVC's Basic Needs

	Main interventions undertaken	Drawbacks/risks	What interventions are more relevant ?
Risk of dropping out of school (education)	– Abolish school fees.	– May create stigma if targeted only to orphans – May not be financially sustainable	Sectoral approach is more relevant.
	– Enact school subsidies (fees, books, uniform) for OVC. – Extend cash grant to guardian tied to child's attendance at school.	– May not be financially sustainable over the long run if not well targeted. – May create dependency behavior.	Yet some OVC may still require some special assistance:
	– Promote alternative forms of education: distant learning, community schools, interactive radio education.	– Requires specific training, input, and strong community commitment.	– Provide conditional transfers (on the condition that the child attends school) to the most vulnerable children in the community.
	– Arrange community fund-raising to send OVC children to school. – Arrange community grants by governments/donors. – Collect used uniforms, shoes, books to hand over to OVC in need.	– Require a strong mobilization of community members. – May create stigma if targeted only to orphans	– Liaise with school officials to improve access of OVC to school through waiving fees.
	– Enable OVC to attend school without uniform. – Offer vocational training and informal education for youths.	– May create stigma if targeted only to orphans. – Requires trainers, initial inputs.	
	– Establish preschool programs for children ages 3–6.	– Requires teachers to be trained, external subsidies.	
	– Bring in home helpers to perform household chores. – Initiate economic strengthening to enable households to pay school fees.	– May overburden volunteers.	

(Continued)

Table 4.4 Risks Faced by OVC and Interventions to Help Families Meet OVC's Basic Needs (*Continued*)

	Main interventions undertaken	Drawbacks/risks	What interventions are more relevant ?
Risk of exposure to health risks	– Arrange health subsidies for OVC. – Undertake immunization campaign.	– May create stigma. – May not be financially sustainable over the long run if not well targeted.	Sectoral approach is more relevant.
or missing immunizations	– Distribute medicines to the neediest households.	– May create stigma. – May not be financially sustainable over the long run if not well targeted.	Yet some OVC still may require some special assistance: – Provide the most vulnerable children in the community with free health care and immunization. – Liaise with basic health care centers officials to provide the most vulnerable children with free medical visits and medicines.
	– Establish rural pharmacies.	– Requires initial input. – Requires training (management). – May not reach the neediest.	
	– Establish home-based care, day care center, youth club, hospital referral.	– Requires initial training, medical input, and commitment of volunteers.	
Risk of nutritional shortfalls	– Improve agricultural production.	– Requires technical and material (agriculture input) assistance.	Sectoral approach is more relevant.
	– Enhance effective health and nutrition practices.	– Requires trainers.	Yet some OVC may still require some special assistance, such as free food.
	– Establish feeding programs, food baskets.	– Relies on external assistance. – May create stigma. – May not be financially sustainable over the long run.	

	Interventions	Challenges	
Risk of abuse	– Arrange home visits by community members (volunteers) to monitor the general well-being of the child.	– May overburden volunteers. – Home visitors must be adequately trained to monitor the OVC's well-being and provide material relief when needed. – Insufficient qualified volunteers	Community-based care provided by volunteers is the most cost-effective. Yet the sustainability of their motivation over the long term raises some concerns and must be addressed adequately at the local levels.
	– Arrange home visits by NGO or public health staff to monitor the general well-being of the child.	– Insufficient qualified staff	
	– Raise awareness of OVC's needs.	– Needs leaders' involvement: traditional community leaders, religious group leaders, and political leaders.	Strengthen the capacity of social workers and social services.
	– Establish effective referral system to welfare services. – Enact appropriate legal laws and practices.	– Insufficient qualified staff – Requires leaders' involvement: traditional community leaders, religious group leaders, and political leaders.	
Risk of trauma: psychological and emotional support	– Arrange home visits by community members (volunteers) to monitor the general well-being of the child. – Arrange home visits by NGO or public health staff to monitor the general well-being of the child.	– May overburden volunteers. – Home visitors have to be adequately trained. – Insufficient qualified volunteers – Insufficient qualified staff	Community-based care provided by volunteers is the most cost-effective. Yet the sustainability of their motivation over the long term raises some concerns and must be addressed adequately at the local levels.

Source: The authors.

Because governments in poor countries often lack the funds to finance transfers, the involvement of the donor community is strongly needed. However, it is absolutely imperative that the governments provide some, albeit gradually increasing, matching funds, not only to promote ownership but also to render the program sustainable when donor assistance begins to slip.

Resorting to Institutional Placements When No Other Solution Is Available

Eventually, for those children with special needs (e.g., those who have been abandoned, who are handicapped, or who are HIV/AIDS-infected orphans), placement in an institution (preferably a foster home) may be the last pragmatic solution available. Special attention is needed to ensure that these institutions comply with established standards and norms.

Table 4.4 provides details of specific interventions under the social risk management approach, delineating the many risks faced by orphans, the main interventions undertaken thus far, their drawbacks, and what needs to be done to improve them and render them relevant to the observed risks.

Notes

1. Also see John Williamson's review, "Selected Resource Material Concerning Children and Families Affected by HIV/AIDS," at http://www.worldbank. org/children/Williamson.doc.

2. Plan International and others (2001) provide a very interesting overview of the current good practices in OVC support interventions.

3. Table 4.2, which appears later in this chapter, presents a summary of responses developed at the community, NGO, and government levels.

4. "Among other things" was added here because reducing birth-related mortality is an important factor in reducing orphanhood.

5. Indeed, one cannot expect microfinance to pull destitute households out of poverty. However, for those poor households able to carry out an income-generating activity, microfinance services may help those businesses to survive during crises and smooth out the income flow, thereby preventing the

recourse to dramatic solutions such as removing children from school or selling productive assets (Donahue 2000).

6. Financial services help to protect against risks by (a) providing chunks of money to build assets and better manage cash flow and assets; (b) increasing the diversification and development of household assets; (c) offering a place to store savings safely; and (d) increasing women clients' control over their assets (Wright and others 1999).

7. MFIs hardly succeed in serving the poorest segments of the population. However, some experiences have shown that it is possible to reach poor segments of the population by developing simple organizational structures and providing services that respond to a client's needs. Here, the Village Savings and Loan Programmes developed by CARE International may be of interest—see Allen (2002).

8. For a detailed discussion of these interventions, see World Bank (2003a).

9. The World Bank's Education for All (EFA) fast-track initiative should help beneficiary countries deal adequately with this issue.

10. Initial World Bank activities, which primarily target orphans in the Burundian Multi-sectoral HIV-AIDS Control and Orphans Project (MAOP), were launched in early 2003.

11. The Families, Orphans and Children under Stress (FOCUS) program was launched in Zimbabwe in 1993. "The program is community-based and delivered by local CBOs, using volunteers recruited through local churches. Volunteers are trained to identify, prioritize and support orphan households in the area immediately surrounding their home. Visits focus on supporting the role of carers, assessing material needs, and small-scale distribution of material assistance such as seeds and blankets" (Lee 2000).

12. At least 50 percent of COPE (Community-based Options for Protection and Empowerment) volunteers (in Malawi) are illiterate (Mann 2002).

13. Community monitoring can and should be linked to referral resources such as the district social welfare office and, when they exist, victim or child protection services within the police department.

14. These additional issues were specific to FOCUS (Lee 2000). Yet they may be easily generalized to any similar interventions.

15. A similar situation was observed in the early child development (ECD) component of the Second Burundi Social Action Project, where unpaid mothers run informal preschool education circles.

16. Most comments made in the previous paragraph are applicable here.

17. Teachers are often unaware of OVC's psychological and emotional needs. What they often assume is bad temper or laziness may stem from a child attending school with an empty stomach, feeling uncomfortable sitting with other well-dressed students, or thinking of his or her situation at home. Yet teachers occupy a privileged position when it comes to identifying and monitoring students' problems and needs and improving their self-esteem by acting as a source of attachment and confidence (UNAIDS 2001).

18. Dying parents may require special guidance and help in disclosing their HIV status and talking to their children about death and dying. Again, memory books may be a relevant tool in this regard.

19. Also see Tolfree (1996).

20. This approach is followed in the framework of deinstitutionalization.

21. After the 1994 genocide, the Rwandan government used the media to ask every Rwandan family to adopt an orphan—a step that enabled almost all children to be fostered (Hunter 2000). Although 60,000 children were reunited with parents and a surviving relative, many orphans and abandoned children have been fostered by unrelated families.

22. In any society the social welfare system consists of four main sources of support: (a) family and community-based services, (b) state and private education and health services; (c) social safety nets (fostering grants and food relief); and (d) institutions (orphanages, hospitals). These sources are shaped in part by the availability and quality of infrastructures, the economic sphere, and traditional and cultural norms. As a society evolves, the balance among sources of services delivered varies, reflecting the test of strength among them and their capacity to sustain the delivery of services (Hunter 2000).

23. Effective preventive measures also lie in the reduction of orphanhood through: (a) a reduction in unwanted births; (b) a reduction in maternal mortality; (c) prevention of HIV transmission; and (d) support of PLWHA (Hunter 2000). MAPs usually tackle those issues (perhaps not the first one) through health and education systems support.

24. See chapter 5 for details on the costs of interventions.

25. As noted earlier, volunteers' interventions cover home-based care, psychological and emotional support (counseling), child abuse monitoring, and children's rights advocacy.

Interventions and Costs:
What Do We Know?

A s noted in chapter 4, communities, nongovernmental organizations (NGOs), and governments have put in place various interventions to address a range of risks and vulnerabilities faced by
orphans and vulnerable children (OVC). This chapter will provide some ballpark estimates of reasonably successful interventions.

Methodological Considerations

Interventions vary by the scope of their action (i.e., how many children
are assisted), and the type of care or assistance provided (e.g., school and
nutrition support, effort to trace the extended family, group home) and its
quality. Given the nature of the data and the degree of country
heterogeneity, it is hard to arrive at *cost norms* for different types of interventions. Six difficulties preclude us from deriving such estimates:

1. The small number of observations; very little disaggregated data

2. The fact that most interventions are small-scale, often local initiatives

3. Variations in the type of intervention

4. Variations in the quality of care provided

5. Heterogeneity of the groups assisted

6. Dissimilarities among countries (e.g., South Africa versus Malawi)
   and regions (e.g., rural versus urban).

In view of these data limitations, our aim is rather modest and twofold. First, based on the available evidence we will rank the interventions from the most expensive to the least expensive in a *relative sense,* even after accounting for country differences. Second, for one or two critical interventions—school subsidies and nutrition supplements—we will derive some ballpark estimates for a typical low-income Sub-Saharan country. But before we do either, we briefly review the evidence on scale and costs by type of intervention.

Scale of the Intervention

Most of the initiatives reach about a 100 (lower bound), or at best 1,000 (upper bound), of OVC. Uganda and Malawi recognized the problem of orphans early on. Yet the scale of assistance provided even in these two countries is not impressive. Estimates from Uganda indicate that only about 5 percent of orphans (83,100 out of an estimated 1.7 million orphans) received some sort of assistance from 183 organizations between 1998 and 2000 (Uganda AIDS Commission Report, cited by Deininger, Garcia, and Subbarao 2003). In Malawi, it is estimated that 4.4 percent (44,000 orphans out of 1 million) were supported in 1998.[1] Of the 44,000 orphans, 14,000 benefited from material assistance such as school fees. In the provision of this assistance, 161 village orphans committees, 78 community-based organizations (CBOs), and 47 NGOs were involved (Kalemba 1998). Binswanger (2000) notes that in the Kagera region of Tanzania, where an estimated 200,000 children are orphaned, NGOs provide support in only two out of five districts, and in the two districts they serve, they support no more than 5 percent of orphaned children.

Clearly, urgent steps are needed to scale up and replicate successful interventions, especially in overstretched communities. Doing so requires identifying the appropriate programs that are cost-effective and sustainable over the long term, and being clear about the steps involved and the institutional imperatives (quite apart from financial/budgetary considerations) in moving from limited coverage to nationwide coverage. These issues are discussed in this section.

Program Costs

Almost no cost data are available for interventions floated by community-based organizations, by far the most prolific providers of care. The main reason is that most CBOs do not keep records of costs. Cost information is available, however, for a few of the formal initiatives supported by NGOs, private actors, or governments. Table 5.1 presents cost data drawn from available studies.

Although quite disparate, this information provides some hints on what types of intervention could be cost-effective.[2]

Costs of Institutional Care

Regardless of conditions, keeping a child in an institutionalized environment is financially unsustainable because of the long-term heavy burden it places on the organizations running them (table 5.1). The costs per child per year range from US$540[3] (with donated food) in Rwanda to $698 in Burundi and $1,350 in Eritrea. Placing 1 percent of the 508,000 Burundian orphans in such institutions would cost $3.5 million each year. But this is a lower-bound estimate, because the number of orphans will increase over the years. For most countries of Sub-Saharan Africa, this level of costs per child rules out institutional care as the preferred option for scaling up.

The concept of a children's village was developed by the nongovernmental organization SOS-Kinderdorf International. Data released by the organization reveal that maintaining a Malawian child in an SOS children's village may cost up to $2,400 a year. The high cost reflects in part the exceptionally comfortable environment in which children are raised compared with that surrounding the majority of Malawian children (Bhargava and Bigombe 2002). The cost, then, could definitely be reduced by adapting standards to those of the nearby communities. A study conducted in Zimbabwe showed that family-type homes were 14 times less expensive than institutions (Powell 1999, cited by Phiri and Webb 2002). It was also found that the cost of caring for a child in a foster home was about 10 times lower than that of an orphanage in the Karega region of Tanzania (Ainsworth and Over 1999).

Table 5.1   Cost of Interventions

Country	Type of intervention	Cost per child per year (unless specified otherwise)
South Africa (Desmond and Gow 2001)	Orphanage	$684 from government + own fund-raising; may reach up to $2,400
	Formal foster care (grant)	$312
	Support grant (for children until their seventh birthday)	$84
	Place-of-safety grant (short-term grant of 12 weeks to 6 months)	$1.70 per day
Malawi (Bhargava and Bigombe 2002; Mann 2002)	SOS village (NGO)	$1,704
	Institutional care (Open Arms)	$200 + donation (clothes and toys)
	Home visits by volunteers (COPE)	$1.50–5
(Kalemba 1998)	Day care (group assistance)	$13
Burundi (Deininger, Garcia, and Subbarao 2003)	School and nutrition supplement	$148
	Tracing and reintegrating an orphan	$280 onetime expense
	Orphanage (NGO APECOS)	$689 (in 1999)
Uganda (Deininger, Garcia, and Subbarao 2003)	School and nutrition supplement	$105
Eritrea (Deininger, Garcia, and Subbarao 2003)	Tracing and reintegrating an orphan	$305 onetime expense
	Orphanage	$1,350
Ethiopia (Bhargava and Bigombe 2002)	Orphanage (Abebetche Gobena)	$471
Tanzania (Deininger, Garcia, and Subbarao 2003)	Orphanage	$649
(Bhargava and Bigombe 2002)	School fees (WAMATA)	$40
Zimbabwe (Lee 2000)	Home visits by volunteers (FOCUS NGO)	$5–10 by family $0.10 by visit
Rwanda (Williamson, Donahue, and Cripe 2001, cited by Phiri and Webb 2002)	Orphanage	$540 + cost of donated food

Note: All dollar amounts in table are current U.S. dollars. APECOS = Association pour la Prise en Charge des Orphelins du SIDA; WAMATA = People in the Fight against AIDS in Tanzania; FOCUS = Families, Orphans and Children under Stress.

Costs of School and Nutrition Supplementation

School and nutrition supplementation is a more limited intervention, and thus it is less costly than a full-scale orphanage: per child per year it amounts to $148 in Burundi[4] and $105 in Uganda (table 5.1). Yet, considering the number of children who require such assistance, its long-term financial sustainability remains open to skepticism. Using the unit cost figures just noted,[5] we estimate that Burundi would incur a cost of at least $59 million a year to provide school and nutrition support to 400,000 OVC (mostly orphans) who are believed to live in acute distress, or $15 million if the targeted group is restricted to the 20 percent neediest orphans.[6] A similar coverage of 20 percent of the neediest orphans in Uganda would have cost $36 million in 2001.[7] Therefore, the cost of covering the neediest 20 percent of orphans in 2001 would have amounted to 2.2 percent and 0.6 percent of the gross domestic product (GDP) of Burundi and Uganda, respectively. For the whole continent, by relying on the lower-bound cost of $105 per child per year, an expenditure of $720 million[8] would have been needed in 2001 to cover *all* orphans, and about $144 million to cover only 20 percent of the neediest orphans. Without adjusting for inflation, but allowing for the projected increase in the number of orphans, it would cost $882 million for all orphans to receive school and food supplementation in 2010, or $176 million if 20 percent of the neediest orphans are covered.

Costs of Tracing and Reintegration Programs

Tracing and reintegrating an orphan into his or her community, although costly, may be worthwhile because it is a onetime expense. In Burundi, this intervention is estimated to cost $280, while in Eritrea it amounts to $305. Yet it is important to remember that if families cannot provide adequately for the needs of the child, additional assistance will be required.

Cost of Community Home-Based Care

Community home-based care seems the most cost-effective option. The cost per year of a visit to a needy household in Malawi is only $1.50–$5, and $5–$10 in Zimbabwe. These low costs rely essentially on the volunteer involvement of community and NGO members. However, some models of home-based care, such as hospital-run, home-based care, may not be so cost-effective. Indeed, high transport and salary costs, and the shorter time devoted to patients, make this option less cost-effective (UNAIDS 1999).

All this said, comparisons of interventions based on costs can be misleading if the amount and quality of care provided are not taken into account. Desmond and Gow (2001) completed a very interesting study on the cost and quality of care, which is described briefly in the next section.

Cost-Effectiveness and Quality of Care

High costs may simply denote high quality of care. To make a meaningful comparison, outcomes must be comparable. Desmond and Gow (2001) studied the cost-effectiveness of six models of care in South Africa, ranging from informal fostering to the most formal form of care, statutory residential care. Because the quality of care varied greatly among types of care, the authors relied on two measures of costs to compare the different models: (a) the cost of care per month per child and (b) the cost of providing a minimum standard of care. The minimum standard was based on "survival elements"—for example, food, clothing, home environment, education (fees and uniforms included), hygiene, and health care (medical costs not included). Table 5.2 presents the two measures calculated by the authors.[9]

Table 5.2   Cost-Effectiveness of Models of Care in South Africa

Model of care	Cost per child per month (rand)	Cost per child per month for minimum package (rand)
Statutory residential care	2,938	2,590
Statutory adoption and foster care	609	410
Unregistered residential care	996	957
Home-based care and support	506	306
Community-based support schemes	Failed to meet material minimum	276
Informal fostering/nonstatutory foster care	Failed to meet material minimum	325

Source: Desmond and Gow (2001).

Figure 5.1 Ranking of Living Arrangements for Orphans According to Their Cost-Effectiveness

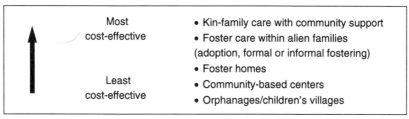

Source: The authors.

Their conclusions confirm that formal institutional forms of care are the least cost-effective models of care, whereas informal models of care, such as community-based care and informal fostering, are relatively more cost-effective, although they failed to meet the minimum standards of care.

Ranking of Interventions

Given the diverse cultural and socioeconomic settings in Sub-Saharan Africa and the complexity of needs of OVC, the need for a continuum of care models is obvious. The available evidence on costs points to the ordering of models of care shown in figure 5.1.

In fact, most countries seem to be adapting the most cost-effective models of care. For example, in Malawi the National Orphans Task Force has developed a guideline on orphan care in which community-based programs are at the frontline of interventions, followed by foster care; institutional care is the last-resort option, as a temporary measure.

Notes

1. Unfortunately, we do not have more recent figures. Based on evidence from COPE (Community-based Options for Protection and Empowerment), one of the major programs supporting OVC in Malawi, it is safe to say that the number of OVC supported in Malawi has increased over the last five years. Of the 1,210 orphans registered in 1995–1996 in COPE's catchment areas, 276 were supported. During 1997–2001, the figures went up—30,000 were registered and 10,284 orphans were supported (Mann 2002).

2. Because few countries and programs are covered in the table, it is difficult to make any relevant intra- and inter-country comparisons. As pointed out by Subbarao, Mattimore, and Plangemann (2001), the fact that "interventions often differ in scope, approach and objective impedes a sound comparative analysis even in the same country."

3. All dollar amounts are current U.S. dollars.

4. In Burundi, no health supplements have been integrated into the orphans component of the World Bank's multicountry AIDS program (MAP) because no cost-effective solution was found.

5. We assume a constant unit cost.

6. We have partly followed the procedure used by Deininger, Garcia, and Subbarao (2003), which restrains the targeted group to 20 percent of the double and maternal orphans. We have broadened our targeted group by including paternal orphans as well.

7. In 2001 the estimated number of orphans in Uganda was 1,730,000 and in Burundi 508,000 (UNAIDS 2002).

8. Deininger, Garcia, and Subbarao (2003) have come up with a much lower figure of $252 million, because they have based their calculus on a more restricted targeted group (see note 6).

9. As noted by Desmond (2002) in a later paper, "While such an approach addresses the difference in material care, a number of problems still remain: how should the common standard be selected? How does the selection of standard affect the results? What if the infrastructure necessary to deliver such a standard of care is not there? And differences in non-material care are not assessed."

CHAPTER 6

Issues in Scaling Up Interventions

caling up interventions means expanding the outreach of programs directed at orphans and vulnerable children (OVC) to cover as many OVC as possible.[1] DeJong (2001) defines *scaling up* as "the process of successfully expanding and improving efforts to meet the needs of OVC, which result in an increased impact." Thus anyone seeking to scale up must focus on outcomes and impact and not so much on inputs per se. However, scaling up necessarily implies confronting three issues on the inputs side: (a) the costs of scaling up and the financial capacity of the implementers, (b) organizational and institutional capabilities, and (c) definitive evidence that a particular program intervention has a proven track record of success and is thus worthy of scaling up.[2] In other words, before attempting to expand, one ought to know *who* to focus on, what to focus on, and the *capacity* (financial/institutional) to deliver (DeJong 2001).

There are still no guidelines to the best way to scale up interventions. Yet at the regional meetings on orphans and vulnerable children convened by the United Nations Children's Fund (UNICEF) over the period 2000–03 in Côte d'Ivoire, Namibia, and Zambia, five action points were identified to facilitate an expanded response to the orphan crisis: (a) undertake a national participatory situation analysis; (b) undertake an OVC policy and legislation review and set up an implementation mechanism; (c) hold a national consultation with all stakeholders and develop an OVC coordination mechanism; (d) develop a national action plan; and (e) set up a monitoring and evaluation system.

This chapter provides an illustrative road map of the kinds of issues that must be confronted along the route to scaling up. More specifically, it discusses three major stopovers in the road map that must be made to assess (a) the current situation; (b) the role of community-driven approaches to scaling up activities, including an analysis of obstacles to such community action with particular reference to practical issues bearing on the financial cost of interventions; and (c) the targeting of assistance.

Assessing the Current Situation

An assessment of the current situation should cover the following aspects:[3]

- Magnitude, nature, and intensity of the problem

- Responses developed by the different stakeholders to address the problem (type, scope, effectiveness, weaknesses)

- Identification of reasonably successful interventions that deserve to be scaled up

- Identification of ingredients that would ensure an intervention's long-term sustainability.

Magnitude, Nature, and Intensity of the Problem

This assessment requires collecting information on the nature, scale, and intensity of the problem:

- The nature of the problem

  - Establish the context: war-torn, postconflict, ethnic tensions, high HIV/AIDS prevalence rates, or drought, among other things. The context will influence the type of needy OVC.

- The scope of the problem

  - Establish the number of OVC and its trend over time.

  - Identify changes in OVC's living arrangements (type of caregivers).

– Determine the kinds of major vulnerabilities (education, health and nutrition, work) faced by OVC according to some criteria (age, gender, level of poverty, orphan's status).

• The intensity of the problem

– Identify the ability of families and communities to cope adequately with the growing number of OVC—that is, vulnerabilities according to the OVC's living arrangements, appearance and increased number of child-headed households, street children.

Because of resource constraints, a clear view is needed of the number of OVC who require support. In some countries, geographic mapping of the problem has proved useful to identifying the most vulnerable regions and communities (i.e., those with a relatively higher number of OVC facing major vulnerabilities). Household surveys, censuses, and more specific surveys can provide most of the information required at this level. At the community level, estimating the number of needy OVC will require a community enumeration and assessment exercise. To avoid any stigma for orphans, it is always desirable to adopt a broader definition of OVC.[4]

Who Does What?

A review of the current mitigating responses developed by the different actors will allow team task leaders (TTLs) to assess

• The scope of the needs still to be addressed

• The extent to which some programs overlap

• General conditions that impaired the mitigating responses in favor of OVC

• Alternative interventions that need to be developed.

The actors consist of households, communities, community-based organizations (CBOs), faith-based organizations (FBOs), nongovernmental organizations (NGOs), international NGOs (e.g., Save the Children, World Vision, Plan International, CARE), donors, and governments.

In reviewing the responses developed by the actors, it is important to look at (a) the type of assistance and services provided; (b) the scope of the responses; (c) the effectiveness of the responses (indicators based on the extent to which the OVC's needs are satisfied; (d) and the major weaknesses of the responses—that is, whether they lacked skills, human resources, material and financial resources, or ownership. Moreover, overlapping or missing actions should be noted, as well as any general impairments such as economic and demographic conditions, social/cultural and religious characteristics, access to basic services, laws, and policies.

Identifying Interventions for Scaling Up Via Community-Driven Efforts

Reaching a sizable number of OVC and affected families requires existing approaches or new ones that are simple and cost-effective and that can be scaled up relatively quickly.[5] In general, interventions have a better chance of being sustained over time when performed by the community and local groups.[6] Moreover, the interventions selected and supported by external agents (NGOs, donors, governments) must not undermine or crowd out existing and local initiatives supporting orphans.

Any decision to expand interventions should rest on several factors. Will the expanded intervention be sustainable, cost-effective, and amenable to rapid implementation? How many OVC and affected families will it reach? What is the timetable for expansion? And, finally, what major weaknesses must be overcome (e.g., lack of skills, human resources, material and financial resources, ownership)?

In launching new initiatives, decision makers should consider those that are missing (e.g., laws protecting women's inheritances, efforts to develop day care centers); whether the new initiative is sustainable, cost-effective, and amenable to rapid implementation; the number of OVC and affected families who should be reached; the timetable; and the major weaknesses that should be overcome. Finally, whether launching new initiatives or expanding present ones, decision makers must estimate costs.

Other Prerequisites for Scaling Up

It is important in any effort to scale up interventions successfully to foster an "enabling environment."[7] Doing so requires (a) defining a strict role for each stakeholder; (b) establishing a partnership among stakeholders and initiating national guidelines; (c) securing financing for the programs; and (d) discouraging stigma and discrimination. Hunter and Williamson (1998a) rightly underscore the point that responsibilities among actors must be well defined and ranked to improve a program's efficiency and cost-effectiveness.[8]

Communities and faith-based organizations are at the forefront of mitigating actions in favor of OVC and affected families. CBOs and FBOs are better placed to identify and assess the needs of vulnerable children and orphans, to help in targeting assistance to the most vulnerable, and to monitor their well-being.

Intermediate NGOs are best equipped to provide appropriate technical and financial support to community groups. Where community targeting is the principal method adopted to identify needy orphans, intermediate NGOs (and faith-based organizations) may have to perform "oversight" functions in order to avoid exclusion and inclusion errors in identification.

International NGOs are best suited to offer financial support to and work with local intermediaries rather than to deal directly with communities. However, in postconflict countries direct involvement may be required initially to respond quickly to OVC's needs and to help communities rebuild their coping capacities.

Donors' principal role is to ensure that funds are adequate, timely, and committed over a reasonable period of time so that interventions are sustainable.

Governments' main task is to provide a conducive environment by developing national strategic guidelines, supplementing donor funds with budgetary commitments as needed, raising awareness about stigma and discrimination issues among the relevant civil servant groups (teachers, health and social workers), altering the legal environment toward more child- and woman-friendly laws, protecting the assets of children from being grabbed by others, and developing the appropriate monitoring and evaluation systems, including especially baseline information on OVC and follow-up surveys. A government, by appointing one person to be responsible for OVC issues within the government, would help to raise the OVC cause and sustain and focus efforts.

All actions undertaken should be tailored to local needs. However, there is a consensus that, whenever possible, interventions should first try to strengthen grassroots responses to OVC and turn toward supplementary interventions only when the primary social safety net is no longer sufficient. Box 6.1 describes how several NGOs are trying to do precisely that: strengthen grassroots responses and tailor assistance to local needs.

Box 6.1 The Experiences of FOCUS, COPE, and World Vision

Families, Orphans and Children under Stress (FOCUS). The FOCUS program in Zimbabwe supports community-based orphan initiatives at urban and rural sites in Manicaland. Female volunteers, often widows with orphans, are given the basic training they need to identify and register orphans in the community. At each site, a church leader, together with a committee composed of other community members, runs the program. Needy orphans are identified, regularly visited, and provided with material support to help them stay in their homes and communities. Assistance includes helping children to rebuild their homes and giving them food, blankets, and primary school fees. An important aspect has been identifying ways to support OVC that complement the existing coping mechanisms. Also crucial has been encouraging the more important members of the communities to be involved in helping affected families. This approach has, in turn, encouraged other members of the community to provide support and has been an important strategy for reducing stigma and community rejection (Foster 2000).

COPE (Community-Based Options for Protection and Empowerment). The COPE program established in Malawi by the Save the Children Federation has developed a strategy to mobilize sustainable, effective community action to mitigate the impact of HIV/AIDS on children and families. COPE's main purposes are (a) to catalyze the formation of community care coalitions in efforts to respond to the needs of children and families affected by HIV/AIDS, and (b) to strengthen the capacity of these coalitions through the appropriate training to mobilize internal resources, access external resources, and organize village care committees and build their capacity to undertake initiatives intended to assist AIDS-affected children and families. At the beginning, COPE collaborates with village headpersons and volunteers to implement a set of interventions (in health, psychosocial, and economic areas intended to assist AIDS-affected families and their children). This initial phase is supposed to last about six months—that is, the period necessary for COPE to help the community start a community-based care initiative that should continue when COPE phases out (Krift and Phiri 1998). Yet new evidence suggests that a better approach would be for COPE to phase down instead of phasing out to make the transition smoother (Williamson and Donahue 2001).

World Vision (WV) Approach. WV supports community-led home care initiatives in which a coalition composed of concerned community members takes responsibility for identifying, monitoring, and protecting OVC with the assistance of WV. Targeted OVC include orphans, children whose parents are chronically ill, children living in households that have taken in orphans, and other children the community identifies as vulnerable. Coalition members are volunteers trained by WV to provide adequate assistance and care during their regular visits to OVC and their families. The neediest children and families are provided with in-kind support (education, nutrition, health, clothing, and blankets), but also with, among other things, access to safe water, spiritual and psychological support, succession planning, and training in life-sustaining skills. Practical support is also given, such as assistance with basic household tasks, care for the chronically ill, and day care centers for young children. One of WV's objectives is to build the capacity of the coalition by providing training in planning, proposal writing, budgeting, monitoring, and reporting so that the coalition can access and manage external resources in order to address other needs (World Vision 2002).

Notwithstanding the kinds of NGO-led initiatives described in box 6.1, caring for an increasing number of orphans and other vulnerable children places a considerable burden on already stretched community resources, as well as NGO resources. Indeed, some communities and some NGOs may have already reached a saturation point and may no longer be able to respond adequately to OVC's needs. Moreover, initiatives leading to grassroots responses may be difficult to foster in war-torn and postconflict settings, which are characterized by weak cohesion among members, ethnic tensions, and unstable environments with refugees and displaced persons. Supplementary interventions supported by governments and donors are, therefore, required, which leads, in turn, to the next issues: assessing the financial cost of specific supplementary interventions and how to target that intervention to needy groups.

The Financial Cost of Scaling Up a Public Intervention: Illustrative Exercise

Concerns that orphans and other vulnerable children may drop out of school or lack access to health care and adequate nutrition have led to calls for public action such as subsidization of OVC's schooling and nutrition. We illustrate the issues of scaling up for one specific intervention: providing OVC with school and nutrition support.

The cost estimates for school and nutrition supplementation presented in chapter 5 are derived from small-scale, localized interventions. The economic cost per beneficiary may be too high when the outreach of the program is limited to a few, but it could be argued that the unit cost of providing the assistance might fall as the intervention is scaled up nationwide. There is really no evidence on the behavior of costs for any intervention with reference to scale. Using the unit cost figures in chapter 5, we determined that in 2001 the cost of providing 20 percent of the neediest orphans in Burundi with school and food supplementation would have been US$15 million[9] (2.2 percent of the gross domestic product, or GDP) and that the comparable cost for Uganda would have been $36 million (0.6 percent of GDP).

For every type of intervention, similar cost estimates are required to get some sense of the overall fiscal implications of providing support to OVC. Moreover, such estimates will help both governments and donors to assess the quantum and composition of assistance required to address OVC concerns in a given country.

Devolving funds to the local authorities may lower unit costs by avoiding the use of expensive staff, costly transport, and costly design. However, if funds are devolved through several bureaucratic levels before reaching the community, the result may be high overhead costs. Empowering communities or local authorities to choose, implement, and monitor a game plan to bring all orphans back into school may significantly lower unit costs.

Who Should Receive Public Support? Issues in Targeting Public Interventions

Given the widespread prevalence of HIV/AIDS *and* poverty, targeting may become difficult because orphans are not the only vulnerable group.

When close or extended families and communities are strained by the consequences of HIV/AIDS, many children tend to be indirectly affected (Foster and Williamson 2000). Children whose parents are chronically ill (and who are likely to be HIV-positive), children infected with HIV/AIDS, and children living in households that have taken orphans (because of the potential resources dilution effect noted earlier) are particularly vulnerable (World Vision 2002). In some settings such as Burundi, high HIV/AIDS prevalence rates are intertwined with postconflict issues, so that both orphans and other groups of vulnerable children need assistance (see table 6.1).

Nevertheless, because of resource constraints it may be necessary to target beneficiaries. Many questions about appropriate assistance transfers and the way they should be channeled remain open. Who should be targeted—the OVC, their families, or their communities? On what basis

Table 6.1 "Needy Groups" by Setting: Malawi, Burundi, and World Vision

Setting	Characteristics of needy groups
Burundi (Postconflict country, HIV/AIDS) OVC are ranked	Category 1 – Double orphans who do not receive any external support; orphaned child-headed household Category 2 – Children, separated from their parents, who live in refugee camps or displaced children Category 3 – Single orphans who receive no support from their surviving parent Category 4 – Double orphans who are living with very poor families
Malawi (Ethembeni area) (HIV/AIDS) Needy OVC were selected, and a list of the "most needy" was drawn.	– Orphans – Children with no food, no clothes, and no bedding material and blankets – Children who are not attending school – Children with unemployed parents who are doing small jobs for neighbors – Children of mentally/physically disabled parents who are not receiving disability grants – Grandmother not eligible for state pension
In HIV/AIDS affected areas, World Vision approach	– Orphan – Children whose parents are chronically ill – Children living in households that have taken in orphans – Other children the community identifies as vulnerable

Sources: Burundi: PMLS (2002); Malawi: Harber (1998); World Vision: World Vision (2002).

should they be targeted—level of poverty or risks of unmet basic needs? How should a transfer be channeled—cash or in-kind? What would be an appropriate amount of transfer? Should transfers be uniform or adjusted to the needs? These and other targeting issues are critical even as measures to scale up an intervention are being considered.

The idea of directing resources toward orphans when the underlying cause of the plight of OVC is poverty has been questioned recently (Lundberg and Over 2000; Ainsworth and Filmer 2002). Not all orphans are at a disadvantage. Moreover, poor nonorphans may be as disadvantaged as poor orphans. Yet Case, Paxson, and Ableidinger (2002), based on data drawn from 10 countries, provide strong evidence and arguments supporting the idea of targeting orphans directly. They show that orphans are less likely to be enrolled in school than the nonorphans with whom they live. This pattern seems to persist even as the wealth of the household rises.

Even when targeting orphans is considered appropriate, it may create a stigma within families and communities. Stigma could be minimized by broadening the number of children receiving assistance in a household, or, as suggested by Sadoulet and de Janvry (2002), targeting *all* the children at most risk of not being enrolled in school or facing other vulnerabilities. Using Mexican data, Sadoulet and de Janvry (2002) show that targeting based on the risk of dropping out has the particular advantage of being cost-effective.[10]

Transferring resources (in cash or in-kind, such as food basket vouchers) to foster parents may also reduce stigma, but such an approach may not adequately address vulnerable children's needs, particularly if resource allocation within the household is biased against orphans. Family support also may increase the household's dependency on external relief, which could, in turn, create additional problems such as promoting a "commercial" incentive to foster a child. In extreme cases, such a situation could result in children being chased out of the household when supports stop. To avoid these problems and on cost-effectiveness grounds, Sadoulet and de Janvry (2002) strongly advocate adjusting the amount of assistance to the level of perceived need (instead of uniform transfers), but this approach is extremely difficult to implement in much of Africa because of information and capacity constraints.

All these considerations suggest that, to be effective, any publicly funded transfer of assistance will have to be carefully designed, avoiding stigma and adverse incentives. Although it is very important to keep the local context in mind, there appears to be consensus on some specific steps and some general principles for channeling education, health, and nutrition support to targeted orphans. First, the country context is important. Table 6.1 provides some guidance on what to look for under different typologies of country situations.

Four steps are critical in identifying "needy" orphans: (a) assess the initial and current country situation; (b) delimit the geographic zone of intervention; (c) assess community strength and cohesion; and (d) select the "needy" children by working closely with the communities and governments.

Assess the Initial and Current Country Situation

Gather information on the nature and scale of the problem to achieve an adequate understanding of the issue. Data should be derived generally from census and household surveys.

Delimit the Geographic Zones of Intervention

Map OVC Vulnerabilities ("Demand Side Map"). Use the information on the nature and scale of the problem to map those vulnerable regions that show a high prevalence rate of HIV/AIDS or a high level of displaced people or refugees, or that are particularly affected by natural disaster. Then, delimit the geographic zones of intervention—that is, those regions or communities with a high degree of OVC vulnerabilities (areas in which households find it difficult to meet the basic needs of OVC[11]). However, where OVC are widely distributed across the country, geographic targeting should be avoided because it may lead to significant exclusion errors.

Map Ongoing Programs Supporting OVC and Their Affected Families ("Offer Side Map"). It is important to know who does what to address the needs of OVC and fill in the gaps where required. To geographically map ongoing activities, collect updated data on all program activities (e.g., locality covered, activities conducted, and number of beneficiaries).

Target Priority Zones of Interventions.   Compare this "offer side map" with the "demand side map" in order to assess where support is missing, and then target and assign priority to those zones where important orphan needs are unmet.

Assess Community Strength and Cohesion

As described earlier, most of the care received by OVC is given at the grassroots level, by families and community members. Consequently, many of the interventions intended to support OVC are channeled through communities. An important prerequisite to providing any assistance is to assess the ability of the affected communities to address adequately the OVC problem. Community mobilization may be weak, but the community may have the potential to sustain any interventions that will be promoted. Economic and political indices may help TTLs to determine this potential:

- Economic indices of potential

  - Access to economic resources (e.g., land policy, credit-saving schemes, external funds)

  - Access to basic services (e.g., safe water pipes, school, health care, day care services)

- Political indices of potential

  - Cohesion within community members (no specific ethnic, religious, clan discrepancies)

  - Structured community: existence of CBOs, voluntary community workers assisting OVC and their families, community work-sharing.

  - Strong commitment among local leaders (e.g., traditional leaders, religious leaders) and their ability to raise awareness and advocate for OVC and affected families.

Information should be collected at the local level through interviews with, for example, officials, religious leaders, teachers, and community members.

Select the Needy Orphans by Working Closely
with Communities and Governments

Efforts to target "needy" children are usually based on an enumeration of *all* needy children within the community. Such an approach limits the number of abuses (overrepresentation of one group over the other) in the selection process of vulnerable children.[12] Vulnerable children should be selected through workshops and home visits by grassroots actors with the help of external technical support (e.g., from NGOs). Because the number of children selected is often too high, sorting out the neediest children may be necessary even after communities have drawn up lists. Children could be categorized according to the "least/middle/most needy children" (Harber 1998), based on whether the children's needs are fulfilled relative to those of other children in the community. Generally in the study by Harber (1998), orphans were always found among the neediest children.[13] However, nonorphan children who lacked some form of care or were subject to abuse were also considered particularly needy children (Harber 1998; Krift and Phiri 1998). In Burundi, after a census of all needy children, the community developed four categories of OVC (see table 6.1). In urban areas, because community identification is more difficult to implement, it might be necessary to rely on other actors, such as religious bodies or NGOs, to organize the identification of beneficiaries.

The problem of stigmatization of orphans, particularly AIDS orphans, is significant, and its solution requires a systematic approach. This problem is especially important in the context of targeting assistance. At the outset, it is important to avoid distinguishing AIDS orphans from orphans from other causes. Determining eligibility for assistance based on the specific cause of parental death is totally inappropriate.[14] However, it is never easy to provide assistance while avoiding stigma. Harber (1998) notes from his South African experience that enlarging the definition of needy children has "created uncertainties in terms of project focus and made it difficult to get across the message within the communities. Field workers found that while it was possible to generate concern within the communities for the plight of orphans, interest floundered because many of the children identified as 'most needy' were not orphans, but were children of another stigmatized group, single teenage mothers." This problem can be resolved only by resorting to the community groups that are best positioned to assess the

Table 6.2 Alternative Approaches to Targeting Transfers: Advantages and Drawbacks

Intervention	Advantage	Drawback
Who should be targeted?		
OVC	– Likely to increase the OVC's well-being	– May create stigma within the family
OVC families	– Likely to increase the targeted family's well-being	– May have diffuse effects on the OVC's welfare – May create dependency – May attract poor households
Affected community	– Can easily reach OVC	– May not be targeted to the neediest OVC, because
– CBOs/NGOs	– Will empower the community	– CBOs and NGOs may lack organizational management skills
– Religious groups	– Are widely implanted and organized – Are well respected in the community	– Religious groups may discriminate against nonmembers
On what grounds?		
Poverty	– Easy to target	– Not cost-effective
Risks of unmet needs	– Cost-effective	– Difficult to implement
What type of transfer should be favored?		
Cash transfers (e.g., supporting foster grant)	– Likely to increase the family's well-being	– Diffuse effect on the OVC's welfare (money is fungible)
Specific in-kind transfers (e.g., education vouchers)	– Easily monitored – Likely to increase the child's well-being	– May create stigma within the family
General in-kind transfers (e.g., food basket)	– Likely to increase the family's well-being	– Diffuse effect on the OVC's welfare
Uniform amount of transfer	– Easy to implement	– Not very cost-effective
Adjustable amount of transfer	– Cost-effective	– Difficult to implement

Source: The authors.

stigma problem in a given local context. Table 6.2 sums up alternative approaches to targeting. Depending on the country context, the approach that is the least stigmatizing should be selected.

Coordinate Donor, Government, and NGO Efforts—Critical

Several donor and nongovernmental agencies are now engaged in protecting orphans in various countries. Indeed, often several actors are found in the same country, with little coordination or exchange of information. Some target assistance; others do not. Those that do target assistance adopt different methods of targeting, often in the same country. In particular, donors, governments, and NGOs should reach agreement in three areas. First, they should decide who will play the lead (coordinating) role. Second, they should delineate specific roles, depending on the comparative advantages of different actors. And, third, they should adopt a common method of targeting in the same province or region in order to avoid confusion among beneficiaries and to prevent abuse of the system (such as when the same household or beneficiary benefits from different channels of assistance).

The lead coordinating role should be played by an agency currently heavily engaged in orphan protection activities, with some track record of success. Obviously, the lead agency may differ from country to country. Delineation of specific roles depends very much on the comparative advantages of different actors. For example, one agency might be best suited for channeling financial or in-kind assistance, whereas another might be best equipped to provide psychosocial support. Finally, adoption of a common community-driven targeting method is important to avoid abuse of the system (e.g., when the same household might receive multiple benefits from different actors, whereas a needy household might be excluded from assistance from all donors—a common occurrence in the channeling of emergency aid during crisis situations).

Conclusions

Some general principles relevant to scaling up and targeting assistance are worth recapitulating:[15]

- *Sectoral and economic policies* are more appropriate in countries or regions characterized by generally low access to basic services (low enrollment rates, low access to health care and medicines, high level of malnutrition). Waiving school fees and uniform obligations would increase the general enrollment among all children (OVC included) without any specific orphan-based targeting. Similarly, vaccination campaigns and nutrition supplement programs would improve the general health of all orphans and vulnerable children.

- *Poverty targeting measures* are required when the average access to services is high, but the difference in access to services between poor and nonpoor is wide. Subsidizing education, waiving the uniform obligation, and supporting the health and nutrition needs of the poorest children would contribute to an improvement in the welfare of the neediest OVC. In such circumstances, conditional cash transfer programs, with a significant element of self-targeting as appropriate, appear promising, especially in countries where poverty targeting based on an assessment of individual households is infeasible because of information, administrative, and cost constraints.

- *Transfer assistance to orphans* is effective when they suffer from discrimination no matter the wealth status of their families. However, before any transfer occurs it is important to first carefully assess the underlying causes of the orphans' disadvantages and avoid stigmatization while providing assistance.

- *Transfer assistance to the most-at-risk children* (e.g., at risk of not being enrolled in school, of not having access to health care, or of being malnourished), regardless of orphan and wealth status, is appropriate where it is possible to identify the risk patterns (with household data sets, relying on behavioral models and a simple set of identification variables).[16] Some countries in Sub-Saharan Africa do have the credible data sets needed to implement such an approach.

- When it is decided to provide direct financial assistance either directly to orphans or to families fostering orphans, it is highly recommended that a community-driven approach be followed, whereby communities and local authorities, empowered with financial resources, meet with the needs of orphans. Appropriate checks and balances, including oversight of NGOs or FBOs, may be helpful to prevent abuse of community-channeled resources.

Notes

1. Scaling up implicitly involves the notion of replicating successful activities. As stressed by Williamson in his comments on a draft version of this chapter, the notion of scale embraces two approaches: to make programs larger, or to

support the replication and proliferation of smaller successful programs. Although scaling up may be an appropriate strategy for certain kinds of interventions, for others it may not be, and, in some cases, it may even be a counterproductive strategy.

2. These three issues are slight modifications of the issues described in DeJong (2001) for scaling up activities to prevent the spread of HIV/AIDS.

3. This section draws extensively on Hunter and Williamson (1998a, 1998b), Alliance (2001), DeJong (2001), and Williamson (2000a, 2000b). See appendix G for a condensed presentation of this section (checklist for assessing the current situation of OVC).

4. Implementing birth and death certifications will help to monitor orphans without creating any stigma.

5. This section draws on Binswanger and Aiyar (2003).

6. Community-driven development (CDD) is an approach that "aims to empower communities and local governments with resources and the authority to use these flexibly, thus taking control of their development" (Binswanger and Aiyar 2003: 5). Interpreted in terms of CDD, scaling up simply implies building and scaling up empowerment of communities with genuine beneficiary participation. Although the concept is simple and easy to comprehend, the successes of CDD have been few and far between for reasons of fiscal costs, hostile institutional settings, the difficulties many stakeholders have encountered in coordinating outputs and services, and lack of appropriate logistics. In the context of orphan welfare, all these obstacles to empowering communities are very real and need to be overcome. These are discussed in the rest of this chapter.

7. This section is based primarily on DeJong (2001) and Alliance (2001).

8. Yet, in reality, some stakeholders may intervene at several levels.

9. All dollar amounts are current U.S. dollars.

10. Sadoulet and de Janvry (2002) have explored alternative targeting and calibrating schemes for educational grant programs based on the PROGRESA poverty-oriented program in Mexico. Simulations show that by targeting the population most at risk of not enrolling in school instead of all the poor, and by better calibrating transfers to needed incentives (instead of uniform transfers), the program could increase its efficiency by 103 percent—the maximum obtainable theoretical gain.

11. The child and community vulnerability indices are presented in chapter 3 (see especially tables 3.2 and 3.3).

12. Such abuses could arise in countries facing ethnic tension, or where particular groups in a community have some kind of influence.

13. Here "orphans" meant children who had lost both parents and were being taken care of by one or both elderly grandparents. Children who were taking care of themselves (adolescent-headed households) and single-parent households were considered the neediest (Krift and Phiri 1998).

14. Kalemba (1998) discourages the use of terms such as AIDS orphans because they add no value to orphanhood. Moreover, from a practical point of view it is not easy to identify "AIDS orphans" because the cause of death is not always known.

15. Based on Ainsworth and Filmer (2002).

16. To identify those children at risk of not going to school, Sadoulet and de Janvry (2002) have estimated an enrollment behavior model in which enrollment is predicted by the children's characteristics (gender and rank), household characteristics (education, occupation of adults, some dwelling characteristics), distance to school, state dummies, and the value of transfers.

CHAPTER 7

Monitoring and Evaluation

M onitoring and evaluation systems (M&ESs) are effective tools in planning, following up, and improving program interventions and their impacts. Monitoring is helpful in assessing whether a program intervention is using its resources (human, financial, and material) as expected, whereas evaluation is useful in measuring the impact of a program intervention with reference to its stated objective. The purpose of this chapter is *not* to detail the many issues involved in the monitoring and evaluation of program interventions. For such a detailed treatment, readers are referred to the World Bank PovertyNet Web site (http://www.worldbank.org/poverty/), which has links to the Impact Evaluation Web site (http://www.worldbank.org/poverty/impact/index.htm), and Ezemenari and Subbarao (2001). The purpose of this chapter is to provide a short outline of the issues that the task team leaders (TTLs) who are designing programs in behalf of orphans have to bear in mind while deciding on the M&E strategy.

Implementing a Monitoring and Evaluation System

The monitoring and evaluation of any program intervention requires

- *Arriving at a clear definition of objectives that can be accomplished when the program is evaluated.* For example, if the purpose of an intervention is to ensure that orphans and vulnerable children (OVC) enjoy the same level of school enrollments as the rest of society, state that clearly at the outset and collect the needed baseline and follow-up information accordingly.

- *Selecting the relevant targets and indicators.* Keeping the objective in mind, select a few indicators that are simple and SMART (specific, measurable, appropriate, realistic, and time-bounded).[1] Because it is expensive to collect information, it is important to be highly selective so that the M&E process is cost-effective.

- *Implementing an efficient information system.* The first step is to assess the ability of the existing information system to provide adequate information on OVC. In many countries, various sources of information are already available: census data, household surveys, specific surveys such as the Demographic and Health Survey (DHS) and Multiple Indicator Cluster Survey (MICS), ministry-level data, published research reports, and data and reports collected by nongovernmental organizations (NGOs) and donors. Investigators should then ask themselves: to what extent can we rely on these data to get a good sense of the welfare of OVC and of orphans in particular?

If the current sources of data are inadequate or imperfect measures of orphan welfare, a sample survey should be launched to get orphan-specific information.[2] Such a sample survey will produce quantitative information on orphans. It is strongly recommended that such a quantitative approach be supplemented with a participatory approach, because it would present an opportunity to bring key stakeholders together and increase their ownership in and commitment to any intended program intervention. Moreover, the participatory approach would strengthen the sustainability of any intervention.

Additional steps include determining the data gaps, identifying the institutions and individuals who will collect the needed data and delineating their responsibilities, and making decisions on the timing of data collection, analysis of the data, and dissemination of the findings and the final recipients.

The Monitoring Process

Monitoring is a continual process in which information is gathered and analyzed in order to follow up interventions. It also provides feedback on any problems encountered in implementation, which helps program implementers to carry out midcourse corrections in the design of the intervention. Local actors will in general undertake the monitoring, joined perhaps by program coordinators and donors. They will rely on a variety of sources, ranging from information collected during home visits, to national surveys, reports, and research reports.

Monitoring the Evolution of the Situation

Properly monitoring a program or any evolving situation implies relying on many data sources and indicators. To monitor the evolution of a situation over time, Williamson (2000b) suggests that stakeholders regularly gather information on the following:

- The *situation:* epidemic/war/drought situation and its consequences

  - HIV prevalence rate (reported/estimated/projected)

  - Child and adult AIDS cases (reported/estimated/projected)

  - Number of population displaced/in refugee camps

  - Mortality rate/morbidity rate (by age group and gender)

  - National population (number and growth rate)

  - Child population (by age group and gender)

  - Number and percentage of orphans (grouped by age, gender, and orphanhood status)

  - Number and percentage of OVC (grouped by age and gender)

  - Gross national product (GNP) per capita and average growth rate

  - Population in absolute poverty

  - Primary/secondary/vocational school enrollment rate (by orphanhood status and gender status)

  - Immunization coverage (by orphanhood status and gender status)

  - Data on children's nutritional status (by orphanhood status and gender status)

  - Population percentage with access to safe water.

- *Household and community coping mechanisms' responses*

  - Evolution of household head

  - Estimated number of children working on the street, living on the street, in institutional care, foster/adopted by alien families, in child-headed households, involved in commercial sex activities.

  - Average household family size (by type of household head)

  - Household dependency ratio (by type of household head and OVC status)

  - Household per capita poverty level (by type of household head and OVC status)

  - Economic activities of households and main sources of revenue (by type of household head and OVC status)

  - Allocation of food, education, and work within the household

  - Number of households involved in income-generating activities (IGAs), with access to credit and savings schemes (by type of household head and orphanhood status)

  - Number of households benefiting from day care services, home visits, assistance such as food, material, financial, or fees (by type of household head and orphanhood status).

- *Existing policies and laws*

  - Child welfare laws and policies (education, health care, work)

  - Laws on the inheritance rights of widows and orphans

  - Antidiscrimination laws (access to school, health care, work, housing)

  - Laws and policies on street children.

When possible, data should be systematically broken down geographically (urban/rural, regions, communities), because situations are very local area-specific. Updated information is also fundamental, because situations may evolve quickly, requiring the initiation of new and rectified responses.

Monitoring Interventions and Program Development

In addition to monitoring orphans' welfare, investigators should monitor program indicators, especially on coverage and progress. Indicators should be computed on a regular basis at the community, regional, and national levels, and should include the following:

- Number of programs supporting OVC and affected families (by type of intervention)

- Number and percentage of OVC and affected families supported (by type of intervention)

- Number of community initiatives receiving some kind of support

- Number and percentage of paid/voluntary staff involved (by type of intervention)

- Number and percentage of trained staff (by type of intervention)

- Cost per beneficiary (by type of intervention)

- Measurable results achieved. Sectoral indicators will be developed in relation to the type of support given. Here are some examples of indicators that could be used to monitor different interventions:

  - *Education support* (e.g., number and percentage of OVC sent to school, remaining in school, and passing to the next grade; provided with technical and vocational skills; provided with educational material, given grants)

  - *Health support* (e.g., number and percentage of OVC provided with medicine, vaccinations, health visits, HIV awareness, height and weight records; number and percentage of families having access to safe water)

  - *Nutrition support* (e.g., number and percentage of OVC and their caretakers provided with food supplements, nutrition education, gardening tools; number and type of meals per day)

  - *Psychological support* (e.g., number and percentage of OVC and their caretakers provided with psychological support or encouraged to write wills)

- *Abuse control,* including legal needs (e.g., number and percentage of OVC and families receiving home visits; number of child abuse cases reported and resolved)

- *Economic assistance provided* (e.g., number and percentage of families having access to IGAs, to credit and saving schemes, or to agricultural inputs)

- *Housing/shelter support* (e.g., number and percentage of families receiving help to pay their rent and repair their house).

According to a report by the U.S. Agency for International Development (USAID 2002), the main challenges faced in monitoring are the following:

- Identifying OVC and their unmet needs. It is recommended that community groups be allowed to establish their own list of vulnerable children based on their own criteria.

- Identifying those programs that intervene in favor of OVC. Reviews of all interventions that support OVC often focus on those interventions that provide support directly to OVC (such as home visits or easier access to health care services, schools, food assistance, material assistance, or psychosocial/recreational activities). To be exhaustive, a review must not overlook interventions that indirectly support OVC, such as IGAs or credit and saving schemes that may positively affect OVC.

- Avoiding double counts of OVC, especially when they receive different types of support or recurrent support for the same provider.

- Developing quality indicators. Simply counting numbers often clouds the issue of quality of care. Quality standards should be designed in consultation with local practitioners, which is not an easy task. Indicators such as the amount of assistance received per targeted OVC/households, the average time of home visits, or the number of staff trained can be used as proxies for the quality of the programs. Assessing directly the well-being of targeted OVC and families will also provide a sound image.

Two additional challenges apply as well (Harrison and others 2001):

- *The ability of community volunteers to collect records.* Volunteers are in the best position to monitor the well-being of targeted OVC and their families during their usual visits to the households. Yet this task may represent an additional burden, especially for illiterate volunteers. The support of NGO staff may be required.

• *The need to maintain a balance between choosing locally relevant factors and those that can be applied more widely.* Although it is important to ensure consistency and comparability across programs, it is also critical not to lose relevancy at the local level.

In summary, periodic monitoring is important to achieve an accurate and updated representation of the evolution of a situation and to adequately follow up, plan, and adjust actions.

Evaluating Programs

Program evaluation is fundamental to effectively scaling up activities that have proven successful and that reach more OVC. Indeed, by assessing the process and impacts of interventions, it becomes possible to identify whether objectives have been met and what has and has not worked, and then take appropriate steps to improve the final outcome.

Evaluations are usually carried out by external consultants to the program at different times in the project life (e.g., midterm, end, and two years after project end). They generally rely on follow-up survey data, which are compared with baseline data. Evaluations also may rely on questionnaires, community meetings, group discussions, visits with caregivers, and meetings with children.

Evaluating Program Performance

A program's performance may be assessed through the computation of realization rates, which compare the effective outcomes of an intervention with the expected ones (i.e., the initial objectives set). Realization rates should be computed at the program, community, regional, and national levels, and cover (a) the number and percentage of targeted OVC and families supported versus the initial objectives set, and (b) achievements registered in the different subactivities conducted by the program versus the initial targets set (see the sectoral indicators developed in the previous section—for example, economic, educational, health, nutritional, psychological, abuse control, and housing/shelter support).

Evaluating the Impact of Interventions on the Welfare of Targeted Children and Families

Evaluating the intermediate and final impacts of program interventions requires computing the impact and outcome indicators based on surveys of a subsample of households. Working at this level enables collaboration with control groups (i.e., nonorphans and nonfostered siblings in the households), which, in turn, allows relevant comparisons.

A baseline study must be conducted at the outset of a program's implementation to provide the data that will serve as benchmarks. Follow-up surveys will allow investigators to build a panel of data so that they can analyze evolutions, estimate impacts at different times in the project's life, and assess the project's long-lasting benefits and consequences. Yet it is important to ensure that the data are comparable by, for example, verifying that surveys were conducted in the same season or under similar circumstances.

Separate questionnaires should be applied to the targeted household and to the children. What follows is an example of the kinds of information and indicators that could be collected. The example is adapted from Burundian questionnaires that were designed to follow up the activities undertaken under the Multi-Sectoral HIV-AIDS Control and Orphans Project (MAOP) orphan component.

Household Questionnaire (Addressed to the Household Head).   Information needed to assess the household's welfare includes:

- Type of household head

- Household size

- Number of children (biological, fostered), adults, elderly

- Number of sick members (long-lasting illness)

- Dwelling characteristics: number of separated rooms in the house, type of floor, walls, and roof

- Belongings: radio, bike, gardening tools, animals, land (surface, culti-vated surface)

- Sources of income (IGAs, grants, credits, remittances, and so forth).

The ability of households to cope and the effectiveness of potential economic support activities (IGAs, credit and saving schemes, distribution of inputs) can be assessed through the following:

- Indicators computed from the previous information

  – Dependency index, wealth index

- Further questions asked of the household head: *Compared with the last round, how has the situation evolved? (Increased, similar, decreased, do not know)*

  – The agricultural surface cultivated?

  – The quantity of the harvest?

  – The quantity of food consumed?

  – The quality of food (i.e., whether more fish/meet/eggs are consumed)?

  – The investment in the house?

  – The number of children going to school?

  – The ability to buy medicines?

Children's Questionnaire.   Information to assess the impact of the intervention on the well-being of children usually relies on observable aspects such as

- Personal identification: gender, age, foster/orphan status, link with the household head

- Education: If the child is currently enrolled in school, in what program (preschool, primary, secondary, vocational, informal training) and what grade? If not, why? Does the child attend classes on a regular basis? If not, why? Does the child receive external support (e.g., books or material) and make efficient use of it?

- Workload: hours spent on domestic chores and the three main tasks performed; hours spent on economic activity work and main type of economic activity performed

- Health, nutrition, and physical abuse: number of meals per day, number of times child eats fish/meat/eggs per week; weight, height, and nutritional score; morbidity the week before the survey (e.g., diarrhea, cough, or fever); whether the child presents physical trauma (e.g., bruises, cuts, or burns); whether the child is often verbally abused

- Psychological: whether the child receives regular counselling from home visitors; whether the child presents psychological trauma (e.g., sad, aggressive, shy, lonely, happy, dynamic, etc.).

This information will help to assess

- Education outcomes: enrollment rates, completion rates, whether children have abandoned school or repeated a class, work–education trade-offs

- Potential discrimination against fostered versus nonfostered children in schooling, health and nutrition status, workload, and general abuse

- The evolution of child welfare and the ability of the household to cope

- The OVC's unmet needs.

Once evaluators have reached their conclusions, recommendations will have to be formulated to improve the program's interventions and impacts. Table B.3 provides an example of the sequencing of monitoring and evaluation activities.

Notes

1. See appendix H for a more detailed presentation of SMART indicators.

2. See *Child Needs Assessment Tool Kit* (World Bank and Task Force for Child Survival and Development 2001), which provides detailed information on how to conduct quantitative surveys.

World Bank Interventions Directed at Orphans

he World Bank has a range of lending instruments that can be used to assist orphans and vulnerable children (OVC):

- Stand-alone projects directed toward OVC

- Sectoral programs (health, nutrition, education, judicial reform) such as the Eritrean Early Childhood Development Project

- Multisectoral programs (multicountry HIV/AIDS programs, or MAPs, and social funds, or SFs) such as the Burundian Multi-Sectoral HIV/AIDS and Orphan Project, the Ethiopian Multi-Sectoral HIV/AIDS Project, and the Malawian Second Social Action Fund Project.

MAPs are currently the main instruments used by the Bank to support orphans and other vulnerable children. Stand-alone projects for orphans have not been implemented so far.

The overall objective of MAPs is to limit and reverse the trend of the HIV/AIDS epidemic by preventing new infections. Typically, MAP country projects cover four components: (a) capacity building for government agencies and civil societies; (b) expansion of government responses to HIV/AIDS in all sectors; (c) an emergency HIV/AIDS fund to channel grants directly to community organizations, nongovernmental organizations (NGOs), and the private sector for local HIV/AIDS initiatives; and (d) effective project coordination, facilitation, financial management, procurement assistance, and monitoring and evaluation.

MAPs offer a good entry point to assist OVC within HIV/AIDS-affected communities. Indeed, community participation in the development and implementation of such programs is strongly encouraged. Through the availability of external resources and efforts to build the local capacity (often with the assistance of NGOs), communities will be empowered to deal with the orphan crisis.

Interventions in favor of OVC are quite numerous and vary, depending on the project, from reunification with family to home- and community-based care programs. Care and support for OVC and their affected families range from family in-kind or cash transfer programs to day care centers. The types of services extended are provision of cash assistance, food, and shelter (rent payment); payment of school fees and related expenditures; distribution of school uniforms and materials. For capacity building, the main actions take the form of vocational training for youth in marketable skills and sometimes income-generating activities for orphans and affected families.

What Should Be Advocated under MAPs?

Extracting lessons from programs currently in operation remains difficult, because most projects are still in the early stages of implementation. Nevertheless, it can be observed that interventions under MAPs do generally address basic and economic needs, but overlook most of the time the psychological support for OVC (counseling support is generally provided only to people living with HIV/AIDS) and family succession planning. Indeed, after the death of their parents orphaned children are particularly vulnerable to property grabbing and inheritance losses, because wills are not common. Psychological and legal issues should systematically be addressed in MAPs. Finally, because of its HIV/AIDS focus, support to OVC through MAPs has generally been directed only to AIDS orphans, increasing the risk of stigmatizing them. It would be beneficial to broaden the definition of OVC in MAPs to include, according to the local context, non-AIDS orphans, refugee children, and internally displaced children (because of war or drought), children living with sick parents, and children from families who foster orphans (families who foster children often experience fewer resources per head as the size of the family increases, and therefore biological children may see their welfare decrease as orphans join their household).

Challenges

A greater understanding of the outcomes and impacts of ongoing MAPs will provide additional guidelines on what interventions are cost-effective and what type of programs (MAPs versus social funds or stand-alone projects) would be more appropriate in a given context. Social funds seem to be an instrument underexploited for orphan protection (more information can be found on the World Bank's social funds Web site at http://www.worldbank.org/socialfunds). Because projects financed through social funds are demand-driven and call for the active participation of the beneficiaries, SFs would allow a focus on the most critical orphans and vulnerable children without overburdening the current interventions.

APPENDIX B

Tables

Table B.1 Checklist of Children's Vulnerability and Their Indicators/Outcomes by Gender and Age Group

| | Indicators/outcomes | | | | | | | |
| | Girls | | | | Boys | | | |
Vulnerability	0–5	6–11	12–18	Total	0–5	6–11	12–18	Total
Inadequate shelter								
– Type of habitation								
– Loss of property (yes/no)								
Loss of human capital								
– Currently enrolled								
– Preschool attendance	√				√			
– Primary school enrollment rate		√				√		
– Secondary school enrollment rate			√				√	
– Completion rate								
– Literacy rate			√				√	
– Has followed a training course			√				√	
Malnutrition								
– Anthropometrics index values	√				√			
Inadequate health care								
– Access to safe water (yes/no)								
– Access to health care services (km)								
– Morbidity rate								

(Continued)

Table B.1 Checklist of Children's Vulnerability and Their Indicators/Outcomes by Gender and Age Group (*Continued*)

| | Indicators/outcomes | | | | | | | |
| | Girls | | | | Boys | | | |
Vulnerability	*0–5*	*6–11*	*12–18*	*Total*	*0–5*	*6–11*	*12–18*	*Total*
– Mortality rate	√				√			

Exploitation
  – Economic activity workload (hours/week)
  – Domestic chores workload (hours/week)
		√	√			√	√	

Abuse and violence
  – Verbally abused
  – Physically abused
  – Sexually abused
		√	√			√	√	

Lack of care
  – Mother is absent (yes/no)
  – Feels loved (yes/no)								

Psychological trauma – Index								

Source: The authors.
Note: √ = specific to this category.

Table B.2 Checklist of Orphans' Needs by Gender and Age Group

	Girls			Boys		
Needs	0–5	6–14	Total	0–5	6–14	Total
Basic needs						
– Shelter						
– Food						
– Access to health care						
– Clothing						
– Education						
Economic needs						
– Productive skill (training, vocational education)	n.a.			n.a.		
– Income-generating activities	n.a.			n.a.		
– Farm/productive inputs	n.a.			n.a.		
Safety needs						
– Protection from						
– Verbal abuse						
– Physical abuse						
– Sexual abuse						
– Work exploitation						
Legal needs						
– Property inheritance right						
Psychological needs						
– Loving environment (need of attachment)						
– Caring environment						
– Psychological support						
– Socialization						

Source: The authors.
n.a. Not applicable.

Table B.3 Monitoring and Evaluating OVC Component

Method	Time-frame	Responsibility	Objectives	Expected outcomes	Indicators	Recipient
Visits to: –OVC –Caretakers (when relevant) –Schools/ training centers –Local leaders –FBOs –Police and other relevant groups	**Monthly**	Implementing agencies	–Monitor OVC and their caretaker welfare –Monitor the ongoing evolution of the activities targeted to OVC	**Monthly report** taking the form of a standardized sheet of monitoring indicators	Input/ output	–Coordinating agencies
Visits to implementing agencies	**Quarterly**	Coordinating agencies	Monitor/assess the ongoing work of implementing agencies in collecting data	**Quarterly report** synthesizing the evolution of the activities undertaken by local practitioners on the basis of standardized monitoring sheets	Input/ Output	–Authorities at different administrative levels –M&E agency
Meeting –Implementing agencies –Local authorities –Local leaders and other relevant groups	**Quarterly**	Coordinating agencies	Discuss results from the synthesis on implementing agencies interventions in order to improve operations performances and data collection and recording	**Meeting report** with specific recommendations on how to improve operations	Input/ Output	–Implementing agencies –Authorities at different administrative levels –M&E agency
Meetings with implementing and coordinating agencies	**Quarterly**	Specialized agency in M&E	–Identify weak and good performance –Foster performance improvement and adequate data reporting	**Quarterly report** on problems identified in the targeted communities and recommendations to deal with them based on standardized sheets		–Local and regional authorities –National agencies (relevant ministry, NACS, etc.) –Implementing and coordinating agencies

Frequency	Activity	Responsible	Purpose	Report	Level	Recipients
Quarterly	**Visits** to: -Regional level -Coordinating agencies -Schools, caretakers, or other relevant bodies	Specialized agency in M&E	Monitoring of operations	**Synthesis report** on the ongoing evolution of the operation in the targeted communes		-National agencies (relevant ministry, NACS, etc.) -World Bank
Bi-annual	**Visits** to: -Regional level -Coordinating agencies	Specialized agency in M&E	-Comparative analysis of performance -Recommendations to improve performance and operations	Synthesis report on performance by commune and region	Outcome	-National agencies (relevant ministry, NACS, etc.) -World Bank
Bi-annual	**Meeting** with -Regional level -Coordinating agencies -Implementing agencies	Specialized agency in M&E	Discuss the synthesis report on performance by commune and region	Bi-annual report on problems identified in the targeted communities/regions and recommendations to improve operations	Outcome	-National agencies (relevant ministry, NACS, etc.) -World Bank -Local and regional authorities -Implementing and coordinating agencies
Annual	Review	Specialized agency in M&E	Evaluating efficiency of operations	Report synthesizing the evolution of activities over the year and recommendations to improve activities implementation and overall program (including the M&E component)	Outcome	-National agencies (relevant ministries, NACS, etc.) -World Bank
Mid-course of the project	Review	Specialized agency in M&E	Make recommendations to improve operations; take corrective measures if necessary	Mid-term review report	Outcome/ Impact	-National agencies (relevant ministries, NACS, etc.) -World Bank
End of the project	Review	Specialized agency in M&E	Ensure the sustainability of results	Final report	Outcome/ Impact	-National agencies (relevant ministries, NACS, etc.) -World Bank

Source: Based on monitoring and evaluation component of the Burundian MAOP.

The Human Rights Approach

The human rights approach (HRA) is based on the Convention on the Rights of the Child, which has been ratified by all African countries except Somalia.[1] The convention covers all rights of all children—civil and political rights, as well as economic, social, and cultural rights. It relies on four "guiding principles" that are fundamental to the interpretation of all the other rights:

- *Nondiscrimination* (Article 2), "which establishes that children's rights apply to all children without discrimination of any kind, for example on grounds of gender, disability, ethnicity, religion and citizenship"

- *Best interest of the child* (Article 3), "which establishes that in all actions about children, their best interests should be a primary consideration"

- *Survival and development* (Article 6), "which not only prioritizes children's rights to survival and development but also the right to develop to their fullest potential in every respect, including their personality, talents, and abilities"

- *Participation* (Article 12), "which sets out the principle that children should be listened to on any matter that concerns them and their views given due consideration in accordance with their age and maturity."

---

1. This appendix draws heavily on Connolly (2001) and www.savethechildren. org.uk/childrights/main.html. The Convention on the Rights of the Child can be found at http://www.unicef.org/crc/crc.htm.

The HRA is a participatory methodology for planning and programming interventions directed at children, based on the concept of a child's rights. It follows a seven-step process described as follows (Connolly 2001):

1. Identification of children's rights: what would be the minimum standards?

2. Assessment: what is the situation of children?

3. Identification of rights gaps: what are the rights violated or at risk?

4. Causality analysis: what are the causes at all levels of the rights violated?

5. Duty bearers: who are they, what are their roles and obligations?

6. Capacity and resource analysis of the duty bearer

7. Define goals, strategy, and actions: what action must be undertaken, by whom, and how?

The HRA is child-centered, but it takes into account the environment in which the child is evolving. It recognizes that children have rights that entail obligations and responsibilities on the part of the family, the community, the society, the state, and the international community. Indeed, for children's rights to be fulfilled, actions are needed at all levels. Yet the HRA is difficult to use in an emergency situation because it requires time in building commitment among partners.

Assessing the Coping Capacity of Households: A Practical Example of How to Compute the Score

he characteristics of the household and the corresponding scores are shown in the following table:

Household characteristics	Subscore	Value
DEMOGRAPHIC CHARACTERISTICS	If the head is a (an).	
–Headed by a woman	adult male: 0	1
	adult female: 1	
–Number of adults (18–59 years old): **2**	elderly: 2	
–Number of elderly (60 years and older): **1**	child: 3	
–Number of children:		
biological: **2**	Value of the number of	
fostered/orphans: **1**	fostered children: 1	1
→ Dependency ratio: adults/(children + elderly)	1/value of the dependency ratio	$1/[(2/4)] = 2$
ECONOMIC CHARACTERISTICS		
Housing:		
–Housing condition:	From 0 to 4	
roof: stubble		3
walls: adobe		3

(Continued)

Household characteristics	Subscore	Value
—Number of rooms (excluded kitchen): **2** → Occupation rate: number of persons/room (i.e., household size/number of rooms)	Value of the indicator:	2 6/2 = 3
Wealth:		
—If the household possesses:		
house: **yes**		0
radio: **no**	Yes: 0	2
arable land: **yes**	No: 2	0
livestock: **yes**		0
private business: **no**		2
—If household receives remittances : **no**		2
—If household has another income-generating activity: **no**		2
—If the household head or spouse has a formal job: **no**		2
—If the household has been expropriated (property grabbing): **no**	Yes: 2 No: 0	0
COPING MECHANISMS		
—Primary school enrollment: All school-aged children go to school	If all or equal: 0 If none: 2 If biological > orphans:3 If biological < orphans: 1	0

—Comparison of children's workload
   (hours per week)
   The fostered child works more than the
   biological children
	If equal: 0
	 If biological > orphans: 1
	 If biological < orphans: 3
		3

—Number of sick persons living in the family (long-lasting disease): **1**	Value of the number	1
—If the guardian is sick: **no**	If guardian sick: 2 0 otherwise	0
Final score: added values		**29**

This household scores 29. A similar calculus conducted on all the households in the sample enables arrival at a mean score and a ranking, given the type of household (e.g., child-headed household, household with sick guardians, or household fostering orphans), according to its capacity to cope.

Principles for Guiding OVC Interventions

The 12 Principles for Programming Endorsed by the UNAIDS Committee in November 2001 (USAID 2002)

1- Strengthen the protection and care of orphans and other vulnerable children within their extended families and communities;

2- Strengthen the economic coping capacities of families and communities;

3- Enhance the capacity of families and communities to respond to the psychosocial needs of orphans, vulnerable children, and their care-givers;

4- Link HIV/AIDS prevention activities, care and support for people living with HIV/AIDS, and efforts to support orphans and other vulnerable children;

5- Focus on the most vulnerable children and communities, not only those orphaned by AIDS;

6- Give particular attention to the roles of boys and girls, and men and women, and address gender discrimination;

7- Ensure the full involvement of young people as part of the solution;

8- Strengthen schools and ensure access to education;

9- Reduce stigma and discrimination;

10- Accelerate learning and information exchange;

11- Strengthen patterns and partnerships at all levels and build coalitions among stakeholders;

12- Ensure that external support strengthens and does not undermine community initiative and motivation.

Declaration of Commitment on HIV/AIDS of the UNGASS (United Nations General Assembly Special Session on HIV/AIDS), June 2001

Articles 65–67: Children Orphaned and Affected by HIV/AIDS Need Special Assistance

65. By 2003, develop and by 2005 implement national policies and strategies to: build and strengthen governmental, family and community capacities to provide a supportive environment for orphans and girls and boys infected and affected by HIV/AIDS including by providing appropriate counseling and psycho-social support; ensuring their enrolment in school and access to shelter, good nutrition, health and social services on an equal basis with other children; to protect orphans and vulnerable children from all forms of abuse, violence, exploitation, discrimination, trafficking and loss of inheritance;

66. Ensure non-discrimination and full and equal enjoyment of all human rights through the promotion of an active and visible policy of de-stigmatization of children orphaned and made vulnerable by HIV/AIDS;

67. Urge the international community, particularly donor countries, civil society, as well as the private sector to complement effectively national programs to support programs for children orphaned or made vulnerable by HIV/AIDS in affected regions, in countries at high risk and to direct special assistance to sub-Saharan Africa; . . .

How Microfinance Institutions (MFIs) Can Help Mitigate the Adverse Impacts of HIV/AIDS

In this appendix we have reproduced part of Joan Parker's insightful "Discussion Paper: Microfinance and HIV/AIDS" (Parker 2000).

A small but growing number of microfinance institutions have begun to experiment with programmatic changes to address the HIV/AIDS crisis. Looking at their experiences thus far, programming options can be examined in terms of three choices:

- *HIV/AIDS prevention versus mitigation activities:* This choice has much to do with timing of the intervention. If the MFI acts when the epidemic is considered "nascent" (where the prevalence is less than 5% of all known high-risk populations), prevention messages may be what clients most need. At more progressed stages of the epidemic, however, prevention messages may need to be combined with mitigation efforts—those that aim to provide care and support to households affected by HIV/AIDS.

- *Action by the MFI itself versus linkages with other institutions:* MFIs may choose to act strictly within their institutional boundaries or through linkages with non-microfinance institutions. Linkage options range from simple referral services to strategic partnerships. Creation of linkages is often chosen as a way for MFIs to avail their clients of the most appropriate health-related services in the most cost-effective manner. [Yet, although a unified approach cannot deliver as broad a range of services to the poor and a parallel delivery system, evidence shows that the quality of the financial and non-financial services provided is not compromised when delivered by one and the same person to a village bank. In addition, the costs may be significantly lower (Dunford 2001; also see the Credit with Education approach developed by Freedom From Hunger)].

• *Financial services versus non-financial services:* MFIs have multiple opportunities for action even when focusing solely on financial services. Alternatively, MFIs may decide to step beyond the boundaries of financial services, and facilitate or provide non-financial HIV/AIDS services such as training, advice or even healthcare. Non-financial services to MFI clients may provide an important opportunity for a linkage program.

[Combinations of the three choices just presented are commonly observed. Strategies have been classified under two broad categories: HIV/AIDS prevention activities and HIV/AIDS mitigation activities.]

Prevention Activities

To date, the largest number of on-going MFI experiments revolve around providing HIV/AIDS prevention information. Typically using regular village bank or group meetings as a natural forum for disbursing information, these programs create partnerships with HIV/AIDS health specialists to meet with clients, provide information, and encourage safe behaviors. If based on a strategic partnership with health organizations, these programs appear to be relatively straight-forward and low-cost (but not cost-free) to design and implement. They may be particularly valuable if implemented before the disease is widespread and entrenched.

Mitigation Activities

. . . MFI mitigation options can be divided between those related to financial products—which are in keeping with a strictly financial service mandate—

Table F.1 Mitigating Activities Related to Financial Products and Services

Experiments believed to be currently under way	*Ideas believed to be in the concept stage*
Develop new financial products that are particularly helpful for sick clients: lump-sum and flexible savings products; education trusts for minors; emergency loan products; etc.	Create linkages to other financial institutions if not able to offer savings or insurance internally. (These linkages have already appeared in MFIs not specifically focused on HIV/AIDS mitigation.)
Allow a well adult in the household to replace a sick MFI client.	Revise rules regarding clients' access to compulsory savings.
Allow clients to offset accumulated compulsory savings against loan balances outstanding.	Allow younger clients or those newly establishing businesses to use the MFI's services if they come from an AIDS-affected household.
Provide death insurance, in form of burial expenses, cash payment, or debt wipe-out.	
Create small loan program for members of sick person's family.	
Develop pre-paid medical payment products, designed to cover the cost of future medical treatment, drugs, or hospitalization.	

and non-financial efforts, which go beyond financial services. The two tables below outline both on-going experiments and new ideas on financial and non-financial mitigation activities that have emerged within the microfinance industry.

It is important to note that—of the financial product adaptations listed in Table [F.1]—only one involves a strategic partnership: providing linkages for savings or insurance. The other activities clearly fall within the mandate and decision-making authority of an individual MFI. However, these actions may require specific skills, such as those required to develop new products; or they may entail higher risks as rules set up for the MFI's safety are relaxed.

On the non-financial mitigation actions listed in Table [F.2], the first two on-going experiments are being implemented by multi-sector institutions—those with financial service units as well as relief or community development units. In these cases, the MFI has a sort of "internal" strategic partnership on which to draw to provide these high-cost services. The second two on-going non-financial efforts can be provided at lower cost—but are again offered by multi-purpose organizations with an MFI component. Thus far, there are few—if any—strategic partnerships emerging between MFIs and health organizations on this front. This may reflect the lack of awareness on the part of MFIs about both the need for and the availability of non-financial mitigation services for HIV/AIDS-affected households within their client base.

Table F.2 Mitigation Activities Providing Non-Financial Services

Experiments believed to be currently under way	Ideas believed to be in the concept stage
Develop community-based programs for families caring for AIDS orphans.	Work with Village Banks or Lending Groups to encourage mutual support relationships beyond repayment.
Provide health care unit for terminally ill patients.	
Help clients with legal protection in case of spouse's death: inheritance laws and wills, etc.	
Provide training on children's rights.	

Checklist for Conducting a Comprehensive Assessment of the OVC Situation in a Country

Nature, Scope, and Intensity of the Problem

- Nature of the problem

  - Determine the context: war-torn, postconflict, ethnic tensions, high HIV/AIDS prevalence rates, drought, affected countries, and so forth. The context will influence the type of needy orphans and vulnerable children (OVC).

- Scope of the problem

  - Establish the number of OVC and its trend over time.

  - Identify changes in OVC's living arrangements (type of caregivers).

  - Determine the type of major vulnerabilities (education, health and nutrition, work) faced by OVC according to some criteria (age, gender, level of poverty, orphan status).

- Intensity of the problem

  - Identify the ability of families and communities to cope adequately with the growing number of OVC (vulnerabilities according to OVC's living arrangements; appearance and increased number of child-headed households, street children).

Who Does What?

- The actors

  - Communities, households, nongovernmental organizations (NGOs), community-based organizations (CBOs), family-based organizations (FBOs), international NGOs, donors, governments

- Responses developed by actors

  - Type of assistance and services provided

  - Scope

  - Effectiveness (indicators based on OVC's needs satisfaction)

  - Cost-effectiveness

  - Major weaknesses (lack of skills, lack of human resources, lack of material and financial resources, lack of ownership)

- Overlapping or missing actions

- General impairments: economic and demographic conditions; social, cultural, and religious characteristics; access to basic services; laws and policies.

Identifying Interventions That Should Be Scaled Up

- Interventions to be expanded

  - Sustainable, cost-effective, and can be implemented rapidly

  - Number of OVC and affected families that should be reached

  - Timetable

  - Major weaknesses to overcome (e.g., lack of skills, lack of human resources, lack of material and financial resources, lack of ownership)

- Interventions to be launched

  - Those that are missing (e.g., laws protecting women's inheritance; efforts to develop day care centers)

- Sustainable, cost-effective, and can be implemented rapidly

- Number of OVC and affected families that should be reached

- Timetable

- Major weaknesses that should be overcome (e.g., lack of skills, lack of human resources, lack of material and financial resources, lack of ownership)

• Estimated costs

Other Prerequisites for Scaling Up

• Define a strict role for each stakeholder.

• Establish a partnership among stakeholders; initiate national guidelines.

• Secure financing of the programs.

• Discourage stigma and discrimination.

Williamson (2000a, 2000b) provides additional information on assessing OVC situations.

SMART Indicators

SMART[1] stands for

- *Specific.* Indicators are specific when they are clearly and directly related to the objective and occur at only one level in the hierarchy.

- *Measurable.* Measurability means simply that the indicator is unambiguously specified so that all parties agree that it is what it is.

- *Attributable.* Attribution requires that indicators be valid measures of both the *developmental issue* to be targeted and the *changes* in that target that are to be attributed to the operational intervention.

- *Realistic.* Realism has two elements. The first is establishing the levels of performance and change that are likely to be achieved. The second is the cost-effectiveness in both time and effort to track performance. Uncertainty and complexity in projects increase the importance of information and the need for realistic indicators.

- *Targeted.* Targeted indicators clearly identify the particular stakeholder group that will be affected by the project.

A Test for SMART Indicators: Are They Ready?

All the effort required to identify targets and construct indicators is wasted if they are not monitored and used. Constructing indicators is but

---

1. This appendix is drawn from http://opcs.worldbank.org/me/docs/ Performance%20Indicators%202.doc. Parts of the document are reproduced here.

a first step in designing a monitoring and evaluation system that uses them for achieving results. A good monitoring and evaluation (M&E) system for collecting and using indicators can be ensured by assessing the indicators' readiness by means of the following criteria[2]:

- *Readily given.* The primary and secondary stakeholders should find it easy to share information with the implementation team, because such ease ensures that objectives are both relevant and compelling to the target group.

- *Readily gotten.* Data assessing the indicator should be cost-effective to acquire. Indicators are cost-effective when a management information system is able to track changes in them with a reasonable amount of cost and effort. This tracking includes collecting data in a timely manner and in a form consistent with other information in order to inform decision making. No guidelines are available for the costs that should be allocated to M&E systems, but 1 percent of project or program costs is sometimes cited as a benchmark. In many cases, some forms of data collection exist. Use of an existing system is usually very cost-effective, but the data must be relevant to the developmental context of the operation. National statistics, for example, are often quite useful for evaluation, but they may not be relevant to the targeted beneficiary or useful to guide implementation management. A results focus might find regional macroeconomic data of less use than simple measures collected from the target population, even though the former are easily obtained.

- *Readily used.* The indicator is part of the management information system and is used to assess the quality of service delivered. The most common failure is that information is not used to change management strategies.

---

2. According to (OED Lessons and Practice #8: Designing Project Monitoring and Evaluation), the five components of a sound M&E system are (1) clear objectives; (2) indicators for measuring objectives; (3) cost-effective data collection strategies; (4) institutional arrangements for analyzing data and reporting information; and (5) strategies for using information. This is consistent with the issue of indicator readiness.

Information use can be enhanced significantly by addressing two important considerations during design:

- Institutional arrangements should be made during design and planning to ensure that a system for gathering, analyzing, and reporting data is in place. Capacity-building efforts may be required to establish the system.

- Clear statements should be made of the strategies by which the data gathered will be fed into the decision-making process in a regular and timely fashion. Ideally, these plans might specify in advance the contingent action strategies emerging from particular evidence of impacts.

Recap

Indicators should be

- *SMART*

- *Valid*. Indicators should be validated by stakeholders and should measure with reasonable accuracy what they set out to measure.

- *Reliable*. Conclusions based on the indicators should be the same if measured by different people.

- *Sensitive*. Indicators should be sensitive enough to measure important changes in the observed situation.

- *Gender sensitive*. Indicators should be disaggregated by gender when relevant and practical.

- *Cost-effective*. The information should be well worth the time and financial cost of data collection.

- *Timely*. It should be possible to collect and analyze the data quickly enough to permit timely decision making.

- *In-line with local capabilities and resources*. Indicators should not be burdensome for project partners.

- *Build on what exists*. Indicators should draw on existing local data sets or indicators used in other projects.

Internet Resources

World Bank

www.worldbank.org/children/ (orphans and vulnerable children, early child development)
www.worldbank.org/poverty/
www.worldbank.org/socialfunds/
www.worldbank.org/sp/
www.worldbank.org/children/Williamson.doc (John Williamson's July 2002 review of "Selected Resource Material Concerning Children and Families Affected by HIV/AIDS")

U.S. Agency for International Development (USAID)

www.usaid.gov/pop_health/aids/

Displaced Children and Orphans Fund (DCOF)

www.usaid.gov/pop_health/dcofwvf/
www.displacedchildrenandorphansfund.org

United Nations

UNGASS Declaration of Commitment on HIV/AIDS

www.un.org/ga/aids/docs/aress262.pdf

UNAIDS (Joint United Nations Programme on HIV/AIDS)

www.unaids.org

UNICEF (United Nations Children's Fund)

www.unicef.org/aids (UNICEF protects the rights of children, with an emphasis on primary health care and nutrition, education, water, sanitation and hygiene education, and child protection)

www.unicef.org/crc/crc.htm (CRC, Convention on the Rights of the Child)

www.childinfo.org/MICS2/Gj99306k.htm (MICS, Multiple Indicator Cluster Surveys)

WFP (World Food Programme)

www.wfp.org (Through WFP, targeted food aid is provided to vulnerable groups, including HIV/AIDS victims and OVC via food-for-assets and school feeding programs.)

International Nongovernmental Organizations

Working on Orphans and Vulnerable Children
Care International (www.care.org)
Family Health International (www.fhi.org)
Plan International (www.plan-international.org)
World Vision International (www.wvi.org)
Synergy Project (www.synergyaids.com)
Association François-Xavier Bagnoud (www.orphans.fxb.org)
AIDS Orphans Assistance Database, AOAD (www.orphans.fxb.org/db/index.html)
Save the Children Alliance (www.savethechildren.net)

Database, Demographic and Health Survey (DHS)

Macro International—DHS (www.measuredhs.com/data, www.measuredhs.com/hivdata)

Microfinance

Consultative Group to Assist the Poor, CGAP (www.cgap.org, World Bank's Web site for microfinance institutions)
Microenterprise Development, USAID (www.usaidmicro.org/default.asp)
Special Unit for Microfinance, SUM (www.uncdf.org/sum/, United Nations Capital Development Fund)
Freedom From Hunger (www.freedomfromhunger.org)
Small Enterprise and Education Promotion, SEEP (www.seepnetwork.org)

CINDI—Children In Distress

www.togan.co.za (papers from the conference "Raising the Orphan Generation," held in South Africa in 1998)

References

Adhiambo Ogwang, E. 2001. Child Fostering in Kenya. From Care to Abuse. Paper presented at 12th Conference on Foster Care. International Foster Care Organization (IFCO), Koningshof, Veldhoven, Netherlands, July 15–20.

Ainsworth, M., and D. Filmer. 2002. Poverty, AIDS, and Children's Schooling. A Targeting Dilemma. Policy Research Working Paper 2885. Development Research Group and Human Development Network, Education and Social Protection Teams, World Bank, Washington, DC, September.

Ainsworth, M., and M. Over. 1999. *Confronting AIDS: Public Priorities in a Global Epidemic.* Rev. ed. Washington, DC: World Bank.

Ainsworth, M., and I. Semali. 2000. The Impact of Adult Deaths on Children's Health in Northwestern Tanzania. Research Working Paper 2266, Development Research Group, Poverty and Human Resources, World Bank, Washington, DC.

Allen, H. 2002. CARE International's Village Savings and Loan Programs in Africa. Micro Finance for the Rural Poor that Works. http://www.kcenter.com/care/edu/CARE%20Publications.htm.

Alliance. 2001. Expanding Community-Based Support for Orphans and Vulnerable Children. Family AIDS Caring Trust (FACT) and International HIV/AIDS Alliance.

Andvig, J. C. 2001. Family-Controlled Child Labor in Sub-Saharan Africa. A Survey Research. Social Protection Discussion Paper No. 122. World Bank, Washington, DC.

Aspaas, H. R. 1999. AIDS and Orphans in Uganda: Geographical and Gender Interpretation of Household Resources. *Social Science Journal* 36 (2): 201–226.

Bandawe, C. R., and J. Louw. 1997. The Experience of Family Foster Care in Malawi: A Preliminary Investigation. *Child Welfare* 86 (July/August): 535–547.

Barnes, C. 2002. Microfinance and Mitigation of the Impacts of HIV/AIDS: An Explanatory Study from Zimbabwe. Assessing the Impact of Microenterprise Services (AIMS) Brief No. 34, Management Systems International, Washington, DC.

Barnett, T., and P. Blaikie. 1992. *AIDS in Africa. Its Present and Future Impact.* London: Belhaven Press.

Barrett, K. 1998. The Right of Children: Raising the Orphan Generation. Paper presented at Conference on Raising the Orphan Generation, organized by CINDI (Children in Distress), Pietermaritzburg, June 9–12.

Beers, C., and others. 1996. AIDS: The Grandmother's Burden. In *The Global Impact of AIDS*, eds. A. F. Fleming and others. New York: Liss.

Bhargava, A., and B. Bigombe. 2002. Formulating Policies for Orphans of AIDS and Vulnerable Children in African Countries: Report from a Mission to Ethiopia, Malawi, and Tanzania. World Bank, Washington, DC, photocopy.

Binswanger, H. 2000. Scaling-up HIV/AIDS Programs to National Coverage. *Science* 288:2173–2176.

Binswanger, H., and S. S. Aiyar. 2003. Scaling Up Community-Driven Development: Theoretical Underpinnings and Program Design Implications. Policy Research Working Paper 3039, World Bank, Washington, DC.

Bledsoe, C. H., D. C. Ewbank, and U. C. Isiugo-Abanihe. 1988. The Effect of Child Fostering on Feeding Practices and Access to Health Services in Rural Sierra Leone. *Social Science and Medicine* 27 (6): 627–636.

Brink, P. 1998. Adoption Practice in the AIDS Era. A South African Perspective. Paper presented at Conference on Raising the Orphan Generation, organized by CINDI (Children in Distress), Pietermaritzburg, June 9–12.

Case A., C. Paxson, and J. Ableidinger. 2002. Orphans in Africa. Center for Health and Well-being, Research Program in Development Studies, Princeton University, Princeton, NJ, July.

Castle, S. 1995. Child Fostering and Children's Nutritional Outcomes in Rural Mali: The Role of Female Status in Directing Child Transfers. *Social Science and Medicine* 40:679–693.

Chernet, T. 2001. Overview of Services for Orphans and Vulnerable Children in Ethiopia. Report version of presentation at national workshop, Kigali, Rwanda, March 27–29, 2001. April 26.

Chipfakacha, V. G. 2002. Comparison of Orphan Coping Mechanisms in the Old (Pre-Colonial) and New (Post-Colonial) Shona (Zimbabwe), Ndebele

————. 1998a. Responding to the Needs of Children Orphaned by HIV/AIDS. Discussion Paper No. 7 on HIV/AIDS Care and Support, Health Technical Service Project, U.S. Agency for International Development, Washington, DC.

————. 1998b. Children on the Brink: Strategies to Support Children Isolated by HIV/AIDS. U.S. Agency for International Development, Washington, DC.

————. 2000. Children on the Brink: Strategies to Support Children Isolated by HIV/AIDS. Executive Summary. Update Estimates and Recommendations for Intervention. U.S. Agency for International Development, Washington, DC.

ISTEEBU (Institut de Statistiques et d'Etudes Economiques du Burundi). 2001. Characteristics of Orphans. Statistical tables drawn from the UNICEF MICS-2000. Draft.

International Save the Children Alliance. 1996. Promoting Psychosocial Well-Being among Children Affected by Armed Conflict and Displacement: Principles and Approaches. Westport, CT: Save the Children.

Kalemba, E. 1998. The Development of an Orphans Policy and Programming in Malawi. Paper presented at Conference on Raising the Orphan Generation, organized by CINDI (Children in Distress), Pietermaritzburg, June 9–12.

Krift, T., and S. Phiri. 1998. Developing a Strategy to Strengthen Community Capacity to Assist HIV/AIDS-Affected Children and Families: The COPE Program of Save the Children Federation in Malawi. Paper presented at Conference on Raising the Orphan Generation, organized by CINDI (Children in Distress), Pietermaritzburg, June 9–12.

Lee, T. 2000. Evaluating Community Based Orphan Care in Zimbabwe. http://www.hivnet.ch:8000/topic/care/view?60.

Levine, C., and G. Foster. 2000. *The White Oak Report: Building International Support for Children Affected by AIDS.* New York: The Orphan Project.

Lundberg, M., and M. Over. 2000. Transfers and Households Welfare in Karega. World Bank, Washington, DC. Photocopy.

Lusk, D., S. Huffman, and C. O'Gara. 2000. Assessment and Improvement of Care for AIDS-Affected Children under 5. Agency for Educational Development, Washington, DC.

MacLeod, H. 2001. Residential Care. In *Orphans and Other Vulnerable Children: What Role for Social Protection?* ed. A. Levine. Proceedings for World Bank/World Vision Conference, June 6–7.

Makhweya, A. 2003. The Applied Research on Child Health (ARCH). Center for International Health and Development, Boston University School of Public Health. Presented at OVC Workshop, World Bank, Washington DC, May 14–15.

Makufa, S. C. 2001. Community Care of Orphans. http://www.viva.org/tellme/
events/cuttingedge/2001/bestpractice_orphans.html.

Mann, G. 2002. Family Matters: The Care and Protection of Children Affected
by HIV-AIDS in Malawi. Prepared from International Save the Children
Alliance Study on Care and Protection of Separated Children in Emergencies,
October.

Mollica, R. F. 2003. Young Survivors. The Mental Health of Orphans and Unac-
companied Children. PowerPoint presentation at World Bank, Washington,
DC, April 3.

Monk, N. 2001. Understanding the Magnitude of Mature Crisis: Dynamics of
Orphaning and Fostering in Rural Uganda. In *International Perspectives
on Children Left Behind by HIV-AIDS*. Association François-Xavier
Bagnoud.

Muller O., and N. Abbas. 1990. The Impact of AIDS Mortality on Children's
Education in Kampala, Uganda. *AIDS Care* 2 (1): 77–80.

Ntozi, J. P. M., F. E. Ahimbisbwe, J. O. Odwee, N. Ayiga, and F. N. Okurut. 1999.
Orphan Care: The Role of the Extended Family in Northern Uganda. In *The
Continuing African HIV-AIDS Epidemic*, eds. J. C. Caldwell, I. O. Orubuloye,
and J. P. M Ntozi, Health Transition Centre, National Centre for Epidemiolo-
gy and Population Health, Australian National University.

Parker, J. 2000. Microfinance and HIV/AIDS. Development Alternatives, Inc. Discussion Paper, USAID Microenterprise Best Practices (MBP) Project, U.S.
Agency for International Development, Washington, DC.

Parry, S. 1998. Community Care of Orphans in Zimbabwe. The Farm Orphans
Support Trust (FOST). Paper presented at Conference on Raising the Orphan
Generation, organized by CINDI (Children in Distress), Pietermaritzburg, June
9–12.

Phiri, S., and D. Webb. 2002. The Impact of HIV/AIDS on Orphans and Programme and Policy Responses. In *AIDS, Public Policy and Child Well-Being*,
ed. G. A. Cornia. New York: UNICEF.

Plan International, CARE, Save the Children, Society for Women against AIDS in
Africa (SWAA), and World Conference on Religion and Peace. 2001. Hope for
African Children Initiative. Technical proposal.

PMLS (Programme Multisectoriel de Lutte contre le VIH/SIDA). 2002. Project de
manuel d'Exécution. Burundi, February.

Poulter, C. 1997. A Psychological and Physical Needs Profile of Families Living
with HIV/AIDS in Lusaka, Zambia. Research Brief No. 2, UNICEF, Lusaka.

Powell, G. 1999. SOS in Africa: The Need for a Fresh Approach. University of
Zimbabwe Medical School, Harare. Unpublished paper.

Ramphele, M. 2001. Foreword, in *Orphans and Other Vulnerable Children: What Role for Social Protection?* ed. A. Levine. Proceedings for World Bank/World Vision Conference, June 6–7.

Robbins, D. 2003. Orphaning in the Life of a Child. The Zimbabwean Experience. PowerPoint presentation at the OVC Workshop, World Bank, Washington, DC, May 14–15.

Sadoulet, E., and A. de Janvry. 2002. Alternative Targeting and Calibrating Schemes for Educational Grants Programs: Lessons from PROGRESA. University of California.

Schoenteich, M. 2001. A Generation at Risk: AIDS Orphans, Vulnerable Children and Human Security in Africa. Paper presented at Conference on Orphans and Vulnerable Children in Africa, convened by the Nordic Africa Institute and the Danish Bilharziasis Laboratory. Uppsala, September 13–16.

SC-USA. 2001. Separated Children Psychosocial Practice and Policy Project. Final report. Save the Children USA, Ethiopia.

Sengendo, J., and J. Nambi. 1997. The Psychological Effect of Orphanhood: A Study of Orphans in Rakai District. *Health Transition Review* (supplement) 105–124.

Siaens, C., K. Subbarao, and Q. T. Wodon. 2003. Are Orphans Especially Vulnerable? Evidence from Rwanda. World Bank, Washington, DC.

Subbarao K., A. Mattimore, and K. Plangemann. 2001. Social Protection of Africa's Orphans and Other Vulnerable Children. Issues and Good Practices. Program Options. Africa Region, Human Development Working Paper Series, World Bank, Washington, DC.

Tolfree D. 1996. Restoring Playfulness: Different Approaches in Assisting Children Who Are Psychologically Affected by War and Displacement. Rädda Barnen, Swedish Save the Children.

UNAIDS (Joint United Nations Programme on HIV/AIDS). 1999. A Review of Household and Community Responses to the HIV/AIDS Epidemic in the Rural Areas of Sub-Saharan Africa. UNAIDS Best Practice Collection, Key Material, Geneva.

————. 2001. Investing in our Future. Psychological Support for Children Affected by HIV/AIDS. A Case Study in Zimbabwe and the United Republic of Tanzania.

————. 2002. Children on the Brink 2002. A Joint Report on Orphan Estimates and Program Strategies. UNAIDS, UNICEF, USAID.

Uppard, S., and C. Petty. 1998. Working with Separate Children. A Field Guide. Save the Children, London. http://www.oneworld.org/scf/onlinepubs/guide/AAstart.html.

Urassa, M., J. T. Boerma, J. Z. L. Ng'weshemi, R. Isingo, D. Shapink, and Y. Kumogola. 1997. Orphanhood, Child Fostering and the AIDS Epidemic in Rural Tanzania. *Health Transition Review* (supplement 2) 7: 41–153.

USAID (U.S. Agency for International Development). 2002. Guidance on the Use of USAID Funding for Programs Focusing on Orphans and Other Vulnerable Children and Adolescents Made Vulnerable by HIV/AIDS. Washington, DC.

Wakhweya, A. M. 2003. Health Strategies to Mitigate the Impact of Orphanhood. PowerPoint presentation at the OVC Workshop, World Bank, Washington, DC, May 14–15.

Webb, D. 1995. Who Will Take Care of the AIDS Orphans? *AIDS Analysis Africa* 5 (2): 12–13.

White, J. 2002. Facing the Challenge: NGO Experiences of Mitigating the Impacts of HIV/AIDS in Sub-Saharan Africa. Natural Resources Institute, UK.

Williamson, J. 2000a. Finding a Way Forward: Principles and Strategies to Reduce the Impacts of AIDS on Children and Families. Displaced Children and Orphans Fund and War Victims Fund Contract, U.S. Agency for International Development, Washington, DC, March.

—————. 2000b. What Can We Do to Make a Difference? Situation Analysis Concerning Children and Families Affected by AIDS. Displaced Children and Orphans Fund, U.S. Agency for International Development, Washington, DC, October.

Williamson, J., and J. Donahue. 2001. A Review of COPE Program and Its Strengthening of AIDS Committee Structures. Displaced Children and Orphans Fund and War Victims Fund Contract, U.S. Agency for International Development, Washington, DC.

Williamson J., J. Donahue, and L. Cripe. 2001. A Participatory Review of the Reunification, Reintegration and Youth Development Programs of International Rescue Committee in Rwanda. Displaced Children and Orphans Fund, U.S. Agency for International Development, Washington, DC.

World Bank. 1997. Confronting AIDS: Public Priorities in a Global Epidemic. New York: Oxford University Press.

—————. 2003a. Ensuring Education Access for AIDS Orphans and Vulnerable Children: Participant Module. Washington, DC.

—————. 2003b. Operational Guidelines for Supporting Early Child Development (ECD) in Multi-Sectoral HIV/AIDS Programs in Africa. http://www.worldbank. org/children/ECDGuidelines.html.

World Bank and Task Force for Child Survival and Development. 2001. *Child Needs Assessment Tool Kit.* Washington, DC: World Bank. http://64.106.149.11/aidshome.html.

World Vision. 2002. Summary of OVC Programming Approaches. World Vision International, HIV/AIDS Hope Initiative. Monrovia, CA.

World Vision (with support from UNICEF). 1998. Qualitative Assessment of Child-Headed Households in Rwanda. Monrovia, CA.

Wright, G. A., N, D. Kasente, G. Ssemogerere, and L. Mutesasira. 1999. Vulnerability, Risks, Assets and Empowerment. The Impact of Microfinance on Poverty Alleviation. Final report, MicroSave-Africa.

Young, M. E., ed. 2002. *From Early Child Development to Human Development.* Washington, DC: World Bank.

Index

Boxes, figures, notes, and tables are indicated by b, f, n, and t respectively.